English 7–11

Learning to talk, read and write fluently are the most important skills in which a child must engage during their primary years, and are the key to the rest of their school curriculum. This book focuses on contexts for and approaches to the teaching of primary English at Key Stage 2, in the light of the new National Curriculum. Through a series of guided activities, teachers are encouraged to examine their own classrooms as environments for language and literacy development and to reflect upon particular teaching strategies and activities. Key issues covered by the units include:

- an analysis of language and literacy;
- the processes of language and literacy;
- the use of topic work;
- a critical look at classroom environments;
- an examination of the texts which children read and write;
- a discussion of the role of the teacher.

The book will appeal to individual teachers who wish to develop their own classroom practice in language and literacy teaching, and to schools who wish to use it as a basis for their in-service work.

David Wray is Senior Lecturer in Education at the University of Exeter, and has published many books including *Teaching Primary English* and *Literacy and Language in the Primary Years.*

Curriculum in primary practice series
General editor: Clive Carré

The Curriculum in primary practice series is aimed at students and qualified teachers looking to improve their practice within the context of the National Curriculum. The large format, easy to use texts are interactive, encouraging teachers to engage in professional development as they read. Each contains:

- Summaries of essential research
- Transcripts of classroom interactions for analysis and discussion
- Activities for individual and group use

While all primary teachers will find these books useful, they are designed with the needs of teachers of the 7 to 11 age group particularly in mind.

Other titles include:

Science 7–11
Clive Carré and Carrie Ovens

Music 7–11
Sarah Hennessy

Religious Education 7–11
Terence Copley

English 7–11

Developing primary teaching skills

David Wray

ROUTLEDGE

London and New York

First published 1995
by Routledge
11 New Fetter Lane, London EC4P 4EE

Simultaneously published in the USA and Canada
by Routledge
29 West 35th Street, New York, NY 10001

Typeset in Palatino by Solidus (Bristol) Limited
Printed and bound in Great Britain by
Clays Ltd, St Ives PLC

British Library Cataloguing in Publication Data
A catalogue record for this book is available from the British Library

Library of Congress Cataloguing in Publication Data
A catalogue record for this book has been requested

ISBN 0–415–10427–0

Contents

Illustrations

FIGURES

TABLE

Introduction

There would be little argument with the proposition that learning to read and to write are the most important activities in which children must engage during their primary school years. Reading and writing are the keys to the remainder of the school curriculum and any other significant learning which children and adults do. It follows then that the teaching and learning of English assumes an extremely high profile in primary schools.

This book is designed to help readers take a close look at the nature of the teaching and learning of English and to consider for themselves whether the classroom provision they currently make for this is adequate.

The book is not meant to be simply read through. It is designed to be interactive in its approach and readers will be asked to carry out activities and observations as they proceed through the book. It will be useful for readers to have a notebook handy as they work through the book, for noting their thoughts as they engage in the activities. Many of these activities would benefit from being carried out and discussed by groups of teachers and one important use for this book will be as a focus for in-school curriculum development work. The book is divided into ten Units, as follows:

Unit 1: What counts as English language teaching in the primary school?

This Unit begins by examining the predominant vehicle for English work in primary schools, that of project work. It questions what elements in typical class projects can legitimately be counted as English and goes on to discuss opportunities for more deliberate planning in of English activities.

Unit 2: The teaching and learning of literacy

This Unit introduces the teaching and learning triangle which is used as an organising device for the remainder of the book. This is based on the notion that acts of teaching literacy and language involve a teacher and a child, working in a particular context with a particular text (spoken or written). This Unit looks at the triangle in brief as a way of describing and discussing teaching and learning. Its four parts are then used as focal points for the remaining Units.

Units 3 to 5

Units 3 to 5 examine the nature of the processes of language.

* *Unit 3: The reading process*
* *Unit 4: The writing process*
* *Unit 5: The purposes and processes of talk*

Unit 6: Looking at literacy in classrooms

This Unit asks readers to look critically at classroom environments for literacy. Aspects examined are the physical and social environment, the activities the children are asked to undertake, and the actions carried out by the teacher.

Units 7 to 9

The following three Units consider closely the texts which lie at the heart of language and literacy work.

* *Unit 7: The texts children read*
* *Unit 8: The texts children write*
* *Unit 9: Language as text: structures and variety*

Unit 10: From learning to teaching

This Unit considers the role of the teacher of literacy and language. It discusses insights to be gleaned from recent research into learning and goes on to examine the implications of these for the teaching process. It then puts forward a possible model for teaching and illustrates this with several classroom strategies.

Unit 1

What counts as English language teaching in the primary school?

INTRODUCTION

According to the National Curriculum, English is one of the three core subjects of the curriculum. The vast majority of primary teachers would probably not want to argue with this classification, feeling that the skills and concepts involved in English language were, indeed, among the most important areas of their work. Neither would there be much dispute among the general public about the importance of English language work. Even though people not connected with schools (apart from having attended one at some stage of their lives) might not agree with teachers about just what were the most crucial aspects of English, virtually everybody would rate this area as deserving a great deal of attention in schooling. This is only sensible: after all, learning to read, write and talk fluently and cogently are essential aspects of what we refer to as 'being educated'. They are also vital skills to possess when it comes to finding a job in post-industrial society.

Accordingly, it might be expected that activities which were explicitly labelled as English language work should account for a very large proportion of the teaching time in primary schools in particular. This is undoubtedly the case, and research studies of the allocation of curriculum time in primary schools suggest that between 25 and 50 per cent of classroom time tends to be devoted to activities which count as English (reading, writing, talking and listening). It is also true, however, that, especially in junior schools, there is a great deal of 'double counting' in parcelling up the curriculum between its constituent subjects. Units of work labelled chiefly as, say, History, may also be expected to account for a good deal of English language teaching as well. Almost invariably, when primary school work is organised around the ubiquitous 'project', it will be expected that the teaching of English language will play a major role by being embedded in the teaching of other subjects.

In this Unit, I shall try to open up this idea of embedding English language work into projects and examine to what extent it might be possible to do justice to the English elements of integrated work. One of the major points I shall make is that it is essential, if English language work is to receive the level of attention it deserves and needs, that schools and teachers take a deliberate approach to planning it into their project work, in whatever area of the curriculum this is located.

LOOKING CLOSELY AT A PROJECT: A CASE STUDY

The first step to take is to look fairly searchingly at what actually happens in the planning and implementation of project work and to examine just how salient English language activities are in this. To do this we will analyse the unit of work planned and executed by one teacher of Year 5 children (9–10 year olds).

The unit of work was 'The Ancient Greeks' and the teacher began her planning by using the familiar tool of the topic web. Figure 1.1 is a representation of the topic web she produced for this topic.

The teacher's next step was to go through each of her identified sub-topics and to list the learning activities she wanted her children to undertake as part of their study of each area of content. Under Greek life, for example, she identified the following activities:

Greek food

- Finding out what Greek food was and is like (reference books)
- Watching video and writing accounts of Greek meals
- Planning a Greek meal
- Tasting Greek food, pitta bread, taramasalata, olives etc.

Greek customs

- Watching video about Greek home life
- Reference book work on Greek home life
- The roles of men and women
- Designing and producing posters to show clothes worn
- The role of the slave

Greek education

- Video on Greek schooling
- Different experiences of boys and girls
- Reading children's accounts of schooling

The teacher then planned the ways the class would progress through the project and made a rough schedule of when she hoped to focus on the various sub-topics she had identified.

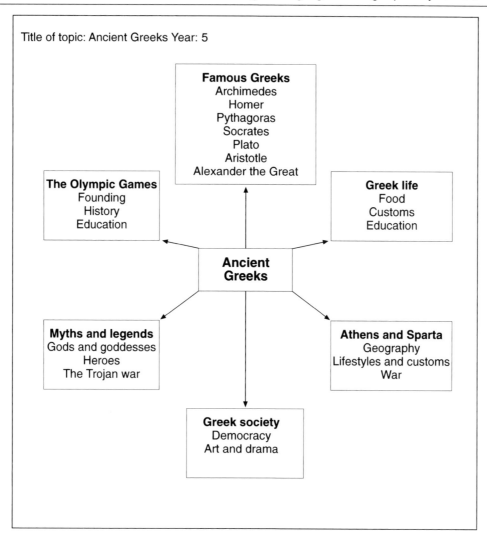

Title of topic: Ancient Greeks   Year: 5

Famous Greeks
Archimedes
Homer
Pythagoras
Socrates
Plato
Aristotle
Alexander the Great

The Olympic Games
Founding
History
Education

Greek life
Food
Customs
Education

**Ancient
Greeks**

Myths and legends
Gods and goddesses
Heroes
The Trojan war

Athens and Sparta
Geography
Lifestyles and customs
War

Greek society
Democracy
Art and drama

Figure 1.1 The Ancient Greeks

To most she planned to devote a defined period of time, usually one or two weeks, before moving on to the next sub-topic. In the case of myths and legends, however, she planned to read these to her class and use them as focal points for discussion, writing and some drama work over the whole period of the project.

ANALYSING THE CASE STUDY

It is certainly not my intention here to criticise this teacher on account of her planning, which, in many ways, was thorough and allowed for a wide range of child activity. Clearly the dominant influence on this planning was the constraint of National Curriculum demands, especially in the History area. The question I want to focus on here is the place and status in this project of activities which can be labelled English language work. You might like, before you read further, to give some thought yourself to this issue.

 ACTIVITY 1.1

Write some brief notes here in answer to these questions.

1   What English activities do you think these children were engaged in during this project?
2   Can you think of other English activities which you might have planned in for them?
3   How systematic an approach to English work do you feel this project planning method represents?

 COMMENTS 1.1

On the face of it it seems that these children will have experienced a fair range of activities which could be counted as English language. They will have:

- Read for enjoyment (myths and legends)
- Read for information (about Alexander the Great etc.)
- Practised reference and library skills (finding out ...)
- Discussed their reading and used it in various ways (Drama, Writing, Art etc.)
- Listened to stories and discussed these afterwards
- Listened to and viewed video material and responded to it
- Engaged in collaborative discussion about their work and the topic
- Wrote creatively (retelling myths)
- Wrote informatively (producing accounts of what they had learnt)
- Wrote for publication (e.g. class books) and, thus, drafted and proof-read their writing

You may, of course, have identified other opportunities for English language work in this project which the teacher appears not to have developed, but this list of activities represents a substantial English component to the work on this project. To suggest that English as a subject was not being well-served by such an approach to project work might, therefore, appear simply as carping.

Yet I feel it is legitimate to ask about the status of English language work when it is, as in this example, essentially an afterthought to the main work of the project. These English language activities arise because they *happen* to fit in with activities which are planned to cover the demands of a History unit of work. In other words, the English language component in this project is incidental rather than an influence on project planning from the beginning.

The problem with activities which are incidental is threefold:

- Incidental can easily mean accidental, that is, not really planned at all. The accidental occurrence of activities aimed at developing a crucial, arguably *the* most crucial, area of the curriculum, seems to do rather less than proper justice to this area.
- Activities which are incidental tend to be perceived as such by the children engaged in them. From the children's points of view in a project such as that described here what they are actually doing is History. The fact that it may, incidentally, involve them in English language work, may well be lost on them. Children's perceptions of what they are doing have a very important influence on their effort and, ultimately, their learning and, if we wish children to give English language work the same priority as teachers and society at large, we have to make sure they are aware of when they are engaged in it.
- One of the constant features of the role of the teacher is the monitoring and assessment of children's progress. This is an essential component of well planned and targeted teaching. If the English language activities which feature in a project are incidental and planned as afterthoughts, then the teacher's assessment of children's performance in them is likely to be the same. This is simply not adequate. It is surely more important for teachers to make accurate assessments of children's progress in reading and writing, for example, than of the development of their historical knowledge.

For these reasons it seems that a very beneficial approach to project work might be to consider the place within it of English language activities at a much earlier stage in planning. If the project can be constructed around the children's needs in English language work, rather than vice versa, it seems more likely that the English language components will get the priority they need. Ways of approaching this will be discussed in the next section of this Unit.

PROJECT WORK AND THE TEACHING OF ENGLISH LANGUAGE

In planning the way in which English teaching might be linked in with project work, there seem to be three basic approaches which can be taken. In the following description of the main features of each of these approaches, you might keep in mind the need already identified to maintain the status of English language work and ask whether any of these approaches meets this.

Approach 1: the sequential approach

In this approach project work is seen as an opportunity for children to put to purposeful use the English language skills they have already been taught. Project work, therefore, has to follow English language skills work and thus be separate from it. The approach, therefore, involves the systematic teaching of English language (and other) skills in the time leading up to the involvement of children in a piece of project work in which they are expected to use and practise the skills they have just learned.

Approach 2: the integrated approach

In this approach the teacher uses the project as a vehicle for the teaching of English language skills. This is done because it is felt that such skills can only be really learnt if the children see for themselves that they are useful, and if they are set in a practical, purposeful context from the very beginning. The Ancient Greek project described above is an example of this approach in action, although it can be carried out in a way which allows for more systematic planning of English language skills.

Approach 3: the concurrent approach

In this approach an attempt is made to teach English language skills alongside their use in project work. Thus the work of the class will be planned so that they receive lessons covering various English language skills at times during the week and at other times they are expected to use these skills in their project sessions. This approach allows the skills to be taught systematically and in the structured way many teachers will be familiar with. It also allows children to have opportunities to use the skills in real contexts and for real purposes as they are being taught, thus hopefully avoiding the problems of children forgetting or being unable to transfer skills.

It is quite likely that one of these approaches is the one which you currently favour in your planning of project work – and they each have their strengths. Spend a little time now thinking about what the strengths and weaknesses of each approach might be.

   ACTIVITY 1.2

Before reading further, try to answer the questions below with reference to each of these three approaches to project work and English language skills.

1   What is likely to be the status in this approach of English language work in comparison to work on other curriculum areas?

- The sequential approach
- The integrated approach
- The concurrent approach

2   Is this approach likely to cause any problems in terms of the scope and nature of children's learning of English language skills?

- The sequential approach
- The integrated approach
- The concurrent approach

3   What possible strengths does this approach have as a vehicle for the teaching of English language?

- The sequential approach
- The integrated approach
- The concurrent approach

APPROACH 1: THE SEQUENTIAL APPROACH

This approach has several implications:

- Because English language skills teaching is given separate and definable time by the teacher, the children will readily sense that this is work that the teacher considers to be important. This approach thus satisfies the demand that English language work be given sufficient status. Yet there is a danger that children will begin to pick up the message that project work itself is less important, and hence less worthy of real effort. The teacher will have to work very hard to get them to see it as a vital and interesting activity, which is how they will have to perceive it if the aim of providing a motivating context in which to practice English language skills is to be realised.
- The English language skills themselves will tend to be taught in isolation. They thus risk being perceived by the children as activities which they have to do because their teacher has told them to but for which they can see little other purpose.
- Because in this system there is necessarily a gap between the teaching of a skill and its use in a project, there is a danger that, by the time they come to the project, children will have forgotten the skills they were taught as language skills. Even more likely, they may not be able to transfer their skills from one context to another. This phenomenon is very common indeed and will be recognised by all teachers. It is seen at its starkest when children spend long periods learning spellings for a test, only to misspell the very same words when writing a story. In project work it may be found that children who can successfully complete any amount of exercises on study skills seem to forget all this when they come to have to use reference materials in earnest. Transfer of learning can be a real problem.

Because of these inherent problems, it is unlikely that this approach will satisfy the aims of those who use it, or be an effective use of project work.

APPROACH 2: THE INTEGRATED APPROACH

This approach certainly avoids the problem of transfer as English language skills teaching is always firmly embedded in meaningful contexts. Children learn as they need to learn. A possible objection to the approach, however, concerns the incidental nature of such teaching and the possibility that opportunities to teach certain skills may not occur naturally. This may lead to certain areas being missed and/or insufficiently developed. This objection can be countered by taking two initial precautions. Firstly, a programme for the teaching of English language skills can be drawn up, which can help to ensure full coverage over a period. This programme is likely to be more effective if it is planned on a whole-school basis, and if it is accompanied by some form of record-keeping. Secondly, in the implementation of this approach, extra language skills teaching can be planned, both to 'top up' that done through the project, and to cover areas which it may not be possible to integrate. An example will help to clarify the approach.

In a project on 'Holidays' with a mixed class of Year 5 and 6 children (9 to 11 year olds), the teacher drew up the following list of 'English language' skills which it was hoped could be taught during the project.

- Reading for details
- Reading critically
- Surveying books and other written materials
- Using reference books and encyclopaedias
- Using telephone directories
- Writing letters
- Writing narrative
- Writing to persuade
- Writing to describe
- Writing personally
- Reading and making maps
- Reading timetables

When planning the project the teacher deliberately included in the plans activities in which these skills would be exercised, and thus taught. These activities were as follows:

- *Reading for details*
  Reading reference books and holiday brochures for details of specific resorts and countries
  Reading brochures for details of prices and conditions of holidays (small print)
  Reading application forms for passports
- *Reading critically*
  Reading holiday brochures and other publicity material for the truth about resorts and hotels etc.
- *Surveying books and other written materials*
  Checking a variety of written materials to ascertain whether they contained information useful at that point
  Using contents and index pages of books

Skimming printed materials quickly
- *Using reference books and encyclopaedias*
Looking for information about countries and cities in the world, specifically concerning their tourist attractions
Finding out about various holiday pursuits, e.g. canoeing, swimming, windsurfing etc.
- *Using telephone directories*
Finding phone numbers and addresses of local travel agents
Finding suppliers of certain holiday goods
- *Writing letters*
Writing to tourist offices to request information
- *Writing narrative*
Writing accounts of holidays real and imaginary
- *Writing to persuade*
Writing holiday brochures to advertise particular resorts
- *Writing to describe*
Writing descriptions of holiday resorts, holiday activities and experiences
- *Writing personally*
Writing personal reactions to places visited on holiday, or experiences had
- *Reading and making maps*
Using maps of the world and ordnance survey maps to locate countries and resorts, and to plan routes
Making maps of various scales to show places visited and written about
- *Reading timetables*
Working out travel times for journeys to various resorts, using rail, bus and air timetables

When children were engaged in these activities, the teacher took the opportunity to instruct children directly in the appropriate skills, using as a starting point the materials arising from the project. It was felt, however, that there were skill areas missing from this work, and these were given teaching time independent of the project work. These areas were:

- Reading for pleasure (this occupied a regular half-hour slot every day)
- Extra basic reading help for those with difficulties (using their usual readers, although several lessons were done using reading material from the project)

APPROACH 3: THE CONCURRENT APPROACH

This is rather a compromise approach which may be welcomed by those who wish to avoid the problems of transfer discussed above, yet feel hesitant about adopting the all-or-nothing fully integrated approach.

An example of this approach will make it clearer. In a project on 'Aeroplanes' with a class of Year 3 and 4 children, the teacher decided that the children would need to use the following skills (only a part of the project is described so that the point can be made more clearly.)

- Reading to pick out the main ideas
- Summarising in their own words
- Handling reference books (using the contents page)
- Writing to communicate information

The activity in the project for which these skills would be required was the production by the children, in groups, of booklets of 'Famous aeroplanes'. This work would involve them in finding information about various aeroplanes in reference books, noting down the main points about each one, and putting this together to write a page or two about each plane. When this was done, they would arrange the planes their group had studied in order of length, attach a drawing of each on roughly the same scale and make up their booklet which would then be displayed for the rest of the class to read.

The teacher began with some work with the class on using reference books to find the information required. She did two or three lessons on this, finishing each with exercises for the children to do in groups and by themselves. After these she introduced the reference books on aeroplanes and did a series of group lessons (because there were not enough books for the whole class to use) on the use of these. The children were then given the task of finding and reading the sections of the books on the planes they wished to study.

While they were doing this in their groups, alongside other normal classwork, she began some classwork on note-taking. After several exercises on this she began to ask the groups to note down things they found interesting about the aeroplanes they were reading about. The next step was to get them to write from their notes, and this similarly was introduced and practised by the whole class before being done as part of the project. The project continued like this, with skills being introduced and practised, as far as possible, by the class, before being used as part of the project.

While this approach may seem to combine the best of both worlds, having both structure and purpose, it does demand a great deal of fore-thought and planning. It is unlikely that approaching every project like this could be sustained for long. In any case, children will differ in their rate of picking up new skills, and it will quickly be found that the class teaching elements as described in this example become ineffective. This will enforce a more individualised or group approach which adds to the complexity. However, this approach does have much to commend it, and it is certainly recommended if the teacher finds it feasible.

The teaching and learning of literacy

INTRODUCTION

One of the things which every reader of this book will have in common is that we were all taught at some point to read and to write. This observation sounds so obvious as to be trite, but it repays some thought as a starting point for a consideration of the teaching and learning of literacy.

Because most people, and, by definition, all those reading this book, are fairly accomplished readers, we tend to think very little about our own learning of the process and the teaching we received. If asked to recall a time when we could not read, most of us have great difficulty in doing so. Our ability seems so natural to us now that our acquisition of it is taken for granted. Similarly with the ability to write. Many people, when asked to think back to a time when they had difficulty writing, will only refer to such experiences as being aware they were untidy writers, or being unable to spell a word. These are only part of the writing process, of course. The more important aspect, understanding the purpose of and being able to make meaningful symbols which can be read back, is often, like reading, taken for granted. Yet, at some point in our lives, all of us were given lengthy lessons, often repeated many times, in reading and writing. We were *taught* to read and write.

Some readers may object at this point, arguing that they could actually read before they reached school age, having 'picked it up' from their surroundings and from those who had cared for them in their early lives. They were not, they will argue, *taught* to read; they just *learned* it. This argument has been taken several steps further by some proponents of what might, often rather unfairly, be labelled a 'caught not taught' approach to literacy learning. Such an approach stresses the environments for literacy learning which teachers, classrooms and schools might provide, reasoning that a literate environment, rich in print and functioning as a community of literate people, will result in schoolchildren learning many of the important lessons about literacy which other children learn in their homes. We shall look more closely at this issue of literacy environments in Unit 4, but for the moment I want to put a different slant on the argument.

The fact is that environments, surroundings and communities are just as much *teachers* as are those people specially employed with that title. The only difference lies in their intentions. Teachers in schools set out with the intention that their pupils will learn and usually have some fairly well developed notion of what they will learn. Those who create and form part of the out-of-school environments in which children also learn usually have no developed intention of causing any particular learning. Yet cause it they do, in a way which meets all criteria for teaching with the exception of intentionality. For the purposes of this book therefore, I want to expand our definition of the term *teaching* to include unintentional as well as intentional activity which has learning as its outcome. In later units, we shall examine the learning which may be caused by classroom environments and by the texts which are selected for children to use. I shall treat these environments and texts as equally powerful teachers as the people who manage them.

LOOKING AT EARLY EXPERIENCES

Although most people will find the next activity quite difficult, it is worthwhile attempting it as it can highlight very well just what is important in the teaching and learning of literacy.

  ACTIVITY 2.1

Think back to your earliest memories of reading and writing. These may be home or school memories. Write a brief account of what it is that you remember.

At the beginning of their initial teacher training course a group of students were asked to write about their memories of their own first encounters with reading and writing. You might like to compare your accounts with some of theirs.

Some accounts concentrated upon reading and two examples of these are given here.

I don't remember much about reading in the infants school. I think we used Peter and Jane. I remember getting very excited when I brought my first book home from the library. It was the story of Peter Rabbit and my mum had already read it to me at home. I insisted on reading it to Mum, Dad and my older brother that night before I would go to bed. I've still got a copy of that book, although the original fell apart through being read so much.

I learnt to read by reading the instructions for my Meccano set. I wanted to build a crane and there was nobody to help me. I remember struggling with the instruction booklet until I managed to figure it out.

Others concentrated upon writing and again two examples are given.

I wrote a book when I was six. It was all about dinosaurs. We had been watching a television series at school and after each programme we had to copy out some notes from the blackboard. I decided to write about the programmes in my own words at home. My mother still has the book although it's a bit dog-eared now.

We used to write stories at school. I liked to write about ghosts and monsters. I remember my teacher telling me that one of my stories was 'really gruesome' and I pretended to know what she meant. I got my Mum to help me find that word in the dictionary when I got home and the next day I told the teacher I was going to write another 'gruesome' story.

These accounts were fairly typical of those from the whole group and it is very noticeable that what these students remembered seemed not to be the experience of learning to read and write but rather particular texts which they read or wrote. This anecdotal evidence of the influence of texts upon literate and proto-literate people fits with an increased recent emphasis upon the importance of text itself in the development of literacy. Until fairly recently, somewhat surprisingly, text, the essential material of literacy, has been rather neglected in research into and developments in literacy teaching. While it has become a focus of attention since the start of the 1990s, in the process several tensions have emerged which have caused debate among practitioners and researchers alike. Text is back on the agenda but in a fairly controversial way.

In the rest of this Unit I want to place the renewed focus on text into a model of literacy teaching, in which it occupies a central place. This model helps to explain the relationships between the various factors involved in the teaching and learning of literacy and I shall use it as an organiser to which subsequent Units of this book will refer. I have called the model 'the teaching and learning triangle'.

THE TEACHING AND LEARNING TRIANGLE

Figure 2.1 represents the teaching and learning of literacy as a three cornered model with text at its centre. According to the model, basically, the teacher teaches the child to read and write in a particular instructional, usually classroom, context and using particular texts.

Our understandings about each of the parts of this model are now substantial. Subsequent Units will look at each of these parts in more detail but a brief outline at this point will help to orientate readers to the kinds of issues which will be discussed.

The child as language learner and user

We now know a good deal about what reading and writing actually involve for the child and this emphasis upon the processes of literacy is in itself a significant shift from a previous concentration upon the products of reading and writing. We have learnt that these processes are influenced by and to some extent depend upon the purposes for which they are carried out, and we have begun to examine the perceptions children have about these purposes (Medwell, 1990).

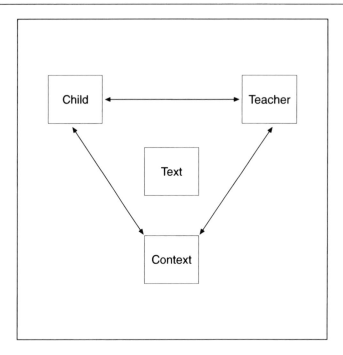

Figure 2.1 The teaching and learning triangle

The role of the teacher

The role of the teacher has come under considerable scrutiny and there has been a discernible shift in emphasis from foregrounding the teacher as an instructor to widening the role to include teacher as facilitator, teacher as audience, teacher as model and teacher as co-participant. This shift has coincided with a reconception of the learning process as a social construction of knowledge. The upshot of this change has been that more stress is now placed upon teaching as providing appropriate conditions for learning (Wray *et al.* 1989), which brings us to the role of context.

Contexts for learning

Of the three corners of the triangle there has, perhaps, been greatest emphasis recently upon context, in the sense of an environment for learning. Stress has been placed upon the provision of demonstrations of literacy, upon the creation of atmospheres in which children feel safe to learn through experimentation and in which they get regular practice of using literacy for real purposes, and upon the careful structuring of support for children ('scaffolding' in Bruner's terms) as they 'emerge into literacy'. The features of this environment for learning have been summed up as 'conditions for learning' (Cambourne, 1988), and such has been the power of these ideas that it has sometimes seemed that teachers have been advised that all they need to do is create a suitable context and children will just learn. The reality is, of course, that the business of teaching is not so simple and it is likely that a suitable context is a necessary but not sufficient condition for the efficient learning of literacy. In any case, it is beginning to become apparent that appropriate contexts are not so easily created as all that, or as unproblematic. If context is perceived as subjective rather than objective reality, as the work of Edwards and Mercer (1987) and Medwell (1991) suggests, then there will be as many contexts in each classroom as there are children. Creating contexts will be dependent upon the individual perceptions of the participants in those contexts, which complicates the issue greatly. This idea gives us an important distinction between environments and contexts which is worth thinking carefully about.

The central role of text

In the past there has been a tendency to underestimate the importance of the texts which are created and re-created in the process of becoming literate. As suggested above, the element of text is at the very centre of this process and is shown as such in the triangle. Children read and write texts, teachers teach reading and writing with and through texts, and texts provide a context for understanding, creating and responding to themselves and other texts. Modern literary theory lays great stress upon the idea that texts are never autonomous entities but are rather 'intertextual constructs: sequences which have meaning in relation to other texts which they take up, cite, parody, refute, or generally transform' (Culler, 1981, p. 38). It would be possible to conceive of literacy development as being simply a matter of a progressive elaboration of textual and intertextual experience.

Attention to the nature and importance of text has seemed to stem from two quite distinct directions of interest, which have at times seemed contradictory in their implications. One of these directions might be termed the structuralist as it has involved the close analysis of the structure of texts, from a linguistic perspective largely inspired by the work of Halliday. Chapman (1983a, 1987), drawing upon the framework for linguistic cohesion put forward by Halliday and Hasan (1976), has examined carefully the ways in which text is bound together and self-refers; in fact, at what makes a particular text a unity and not merely a string of discrete sentences or words. Chapman (1983b) has also investigated the degree to which young readers are aware of the range of cohesive ties present in texts and has found that their level of such awareness is a significant element in their development as readers. He suggests that there is a need to take this element of text firmly into account when planning effective teaching programmes.

Drawing upon the analysis of language by Halliday as social semiotic (Halliday, 1978), the group of Australian researchers collectively known as 'genre theorists' have looked closely at the ways in which text structures reflect a variety of social ways of making meaning (Halliday and Hasan, 1989). The implication of this work is that, unless some attention is actually given to teaching children to operate effectively within the genre structures upon which society is based, children are, in fact, disenfranchised from large parts of wider social life (Martin, 1989; Christie, 1990).

The second direction from which interest in text has come might be termed the authenticist, as it has emphasised the importance of 'real' texts, that is, texts written for authentic purposes (as opposed to mere instructional purposes such as reading scheme texts). Several notable educationalists (in particular, Meek, 1988) have pointed out the ways in which authentic texts can teach readers many important lessons about reading and one of the major motivations underlying what has been termed the 'real books movement' has been the superiority of authentic texts to linguistically controlled scheme, or basal, texts. In writing, similarly, authenticity has loomed very large. The process writing approach, inspired by the work of Graves (1983), has placed great emphasis upon children 'finding their own voices' and composing texts which have real importance to them.

The structuralist and authenticist ways of looking at text have seemed to be in opposition to each other with, at times, this opposition spilling over into direct confrontation and unhelpful polarity. Structuralist views have been caricatured as implying a return to dry, direct teaching of textual features, thus reviving suspicions about the effectiveness and lack of child-centredness of grammar exercises. Authenticist approaches, on the other hand, have been caricatured as being structureless and giving no attention at all to developing children's awareness of textual conventions. Both these criticisms rest, of course, upon misunderstandings and their existence is perhaps more an expression of the long-standing clash of educational philosophy usually referred to as 'traditional versus progressive' than of any serious attempt to come to terms with the differing perspectives.

In any case, the two positions do seem potentially to have much in common. In essence they are both concerned with children's responses to and production of 'real' texts. The genre theorists have continually emphasised that textual structures, and thus the teaching of them, only make sense within a context of meaning. 'A functional approach to language does not advocate teaching about language by handing down prescriptive recipes. Rather, it is concerned with providing information about the development of effective texts for particular purposes, and providing it at the point of need within the context of real, purposeful language use' (Derewianka, 1990, p. 5). Both positions, therefore, emphasise purpose and meaning in literacy development.

They are both also concerned with increasing children's control over their reception and production of texts. For 'real books' and process-writing advocates, the issue of children's choice is in the foreground of their intentions. Only by being allowed to make choices about what they read and write, they argue, can children develop the personal investment in the processes of literacy which is essential if they are to engage in real learning of these processes. For structuralists, developing children's control over the ways text is used for particular purposes in society is one of the foundations of their arguments. 'To learn to recognise and create the various genres found in one's culture is to learn to exercise choices - choices in building and ordering different kinds of meaning and hence, potentially, choices in directing the course of one's life' (Christie, 1990, p. 3).

This issue of school texts will be examined in more detail in Unit 5.

EXPANDING THE FOCUS

The discussion so far has focused upon the teaching and learning of literacy and the ways in which the teaching and learning triangle might help explain the factors which impinge upon this. It is also possible, however, to locate the development of spoken language within the triangle and this I shall do in the following Units. Children use talk for various purposes in classrooms and thereby develop their understandings about its structures and functions.

Teachers usually give some direct attention to the development of children's under-standings about spoken language, and classroom contexts influence the ways in which talk is used within them. Talk itself can also be viewed as a text and there is much evidence that the shape of this text, or discourse, is constrained by classroom experiences. The develop-ment of children's knowledge about the text of talk, of its permissible patterns and structures (an expanded view of what used to be called simply 'grammar'), is also a desirable goal for teaching and thus needs to be given some attention in thinking about primary English.

The model advanced in this Unit can therefore be used as a way of bringing together the various elements in the teaching and learning of English. Subsequent Units will explore individual elements in more detail.

Unit 3

The reading process

WHAT HAPPENS WHEN WE READ?

As teachers of reading, this is a very important question for us to try to answer. Naturally, what we believe the reading process to consist of will affect the way we try to teach it to children. We need, therefore, to examine the reading process closely and the following questions will help to focus our examination.

- When does reading begin? Does the process start as our eyes encounter print or does it begin before that?
- Do we read all texts in the same way or is there variation in the process depending on the nature of the text?
- Does everybody use the same reading process (or processes) or is there an individual element to it?
- How do we differentiate between successful and unsuccessful reading?

LOOKING AT THE READING PROCESS

The following three texts are fairly typical of the kinds of reading matter with which adults have to deal in the course of their everyday lives. Text A is an extract from an article in a national newspaper.

Text A

Poor rations and bad taste

Ian Aitken

There is plentiful evidence in the chronicles of Jeeves and his young master that Bertie Wooster was well-informed about pig farming, but there is nothing to suggest that he was equally au fait with matters horticultural. Had it been otherwise, the parallels between him and the present MP for Twickenham would have been uncanny.

Toby Jessell, who occupies that seat in the Conservative interest, is in many respects a dead ringer for Bertie. He even belongs to an institution which is sometimes compared by its enemies to the Drones Club. His normal manner is that of a 1920s fop who isn't burdened with too much furniture on the top floor.

But his speech in the Commons debate on poverty this week – in which he criticised the unemployed for sitting in front of their TV sets instead of cultivating cheap and nourishing vegetables on their allotments – divided him from young Wooster. Not only did Bertie know nothing of allotments; he also had more taste than to insult the victims of poverty.

(Extract taken from The *Guardian*, Saturday, 18 February 1995, p. 24.)

Text B is the text of an advertisement which appears in national magazines (with the product name deleted).

Text B

Behold. A miracle cure from *********.

Please excuse the rather dramatic headline but we have achieved something of a breakthrough in bacon.

Up to now, there have only been two ways to produce it.

Traditional hand salting, where the pork is left to cure naturally. And wet curing, where the meat is injected with salt water.

The latter is much quicker and therefore much less expensive. But like many modern cures it suffers side effects.

After several months considering the problem, we came up with a unique solution. An entirely new method of dry salting.

The result is ******** …s Dry Cured Bacon range.

Because there is no salted water, there is no shrinkage and no problem getting it brown and crispy. As well as cooking like traditional bacon used to cook, it tastes

just like traditional bacon used to taste.
    And all for little more than the cost of the wet cured variety.
    A miracle? Well, the flavour is certainly out of this world.

(Extract taken from *Good Housekeeping*, March, 1995.)

Text C is an extract from a railway timetable.

Text C

Penzance – Plymouth – Newton Abbot – Exeter St Davids – Taunton – Reading – London

Sundays

		IC	E IC	D IC	IC	A R
London Paddington	d	**1935**	**2035**	**2035**	**2215**	**2355**
Heathrow Airport	d	1845	1945	1945	2145	---
Gatwick Airport	d	1811	1911	1911	2011	---
Reading	d	**2010**	**2110**	**2110**	**2249**	**0042u**
Westbury	d	---	2214	2154	---	---
Castle Cary	a	---	2231	2211	---	---
Taunton	a	2207	2255	2234	0054s	
Tiverton Parkway	a	2219	2307	2246	---	---
Exeter St Davids	a	2234	2322	2304	0120s	0427
Newton Abbot	a	2258	2346	2325	---	0457
Torquay	a	---	---	---	---	0645
Paignton	a	---	---	---	---	0650
Totnes	a	2310	2358	2337	---	---
Plymouth	a	**2340**	**0030**	**0010**	**0220**	**0538**
Liskeard	a	---	---	---	---	0623
Bodmin Parkway	a	---	---	---	---	0637
St Austell	a	---	---	---	---	0704
Truro	a	---	---	---	---	0724
Redruth	a	---	---	---	---	0739
Penzance	a	---	---	---	---	**0819**

(Extract taken from *A Guide to Services*, Great Western, 1994.)

ACTIVITY 3.1

For each of these three texts, think about how you would normally go about reading them (bearing in mind that your approach to reading them now is probably not normal since you have been presented with these texts in a rather unusual context). For each text try to answer the following questions:

- What do you need to know before you are able to begin reading this text?
- How do you set about reading the text? For example, where do you begin, in what order do you read the various parts of the text, which parts of the text do you read very intensively and which do you read with less careful attention?
- Is there anything in the text which causes you any specific difficulty in your reading?

You might like to create a table like Table 3.1 to record your thoughts about each of these questions.

Table 3.1 Examining the reading process

| | Question | | |
Text	Previous knowledge needed	Approach to reading	Difficulties
Text A			
Text B			
Text C			

COMMENTS 3.1

If you discuss your reading of these texts with other people, it should become clear that no two people approach the task of reading in exactly the same ways. This makes attempts to define *a* reading process slightly problematic. Nevertheless, each of the questions posed earlier raises some interesting questions about reading.

Text A

There is quite a lot of knowledge which you need to be able to bring to this text in order to make sense of it. Recognition of it as a newspaper commentary article probably triggers off the expectation that it will be concerned with political affairs and perhaps a brief initial scan of the text highlighted the words *MP, Conservative* and *Commons* to confirm this expectation. If you are unfamiliar with the events to which the text refers, it will mean less to you, although the text itself does give an explanation of the events which provides sufficient context for its meaning to be gleaned. You do, however, need to know something about the literary references used in the text. Who were Jeeves and Bertie Wooster? What was the Drones Club? Most of the readers of this text will, of course, know these things, but try to imagine what sense someone would make of the text if they had not encountered the stories of P. G. Wodehouse.

There are also some features in the text which you need to understand which will only have been previously encountered in certain contexts. The use, for example, of non-English phrases (*au fait*) and idiomatic expressions (*dead ringer, burdened with too much furniture on the top floor*) demands a familiarity with certain uses of language which not every reader will have. The meanings of such expressions can probably, in this instance, be deduced from the surrounding context but in this case the process of reading this text will be very different.

Because of the way this article is written it is quite clear that it is not a newspaper report but an opinion piece. Therefore its reading is probably approached in a similar way to other extended texts. That is, the reader may give the text a preliminary scan to try to determine its subject matter. As mentioned earlier, here the words *MP, Conservative* and *Commons* probably give sufficient information for the reader to decide whether the topic is of sufficient interest to be read in more detail. If it is, the reader probably moves on to a different reading strategy. Some readers will read carefully and intensively every word and sentence. More usual, however, with this kind of text will be a fairly rapid skim-read to get the gist of what the text is saying.

Had this text been a newspaper report, skim-reading would have been almost universally the way it would have been read. Because of the manner in which newspapers are compiled, reporters know that their original texts are likely to be cut to fit the space available. The simplest way to cut text is to chop off their last or last few paragraphs. Reporters, therefore, make sure that they give the essential details of their story in the first few paragraphs, which are less likely to be cut. With prolonged experience of newspapers, most readers instinctively know this fact and generally only give attention, if they give any at all, to the beginnings of newspaper reports.

With regard to difficulties, this text does have some language features which may cause problems for readers, such as the idiomatic expressions mentioned earlier. A more pervasive difficulty will be, however, the fact that the tone of the article makes certain assumptions about the beliefs and values of its readers. It is clear that there are certain newspapers in which such an article would *not* have appeared and some readers of it will react against the implicit values. This causes a difficulty because, in order to understand the argument of the article, a reader has to follow not just its logic but its value judgements. If these are rejected, the argument of the article will be much less well appreciated.

Text B

This is a fairly wordy example of an advertisement, which are usually rather more terse in their use of language. It does depend absolutely on the reader supplying, from his or her own knowledge, the connection between the two meanings of the word 'cure'. Such plays on words are, of course, widely employed in advertising copy.

How do we approach this text? Unfortunately for the firm who paid for this text to be written, designed and placed in the magazine, the truth is that most of those who encounter this text will not actually approach it at all. We are so hardened to the presence of advertising material around us that many of us, once we have identified texts as 'adverts', scarcely give them a second glance. Advertisers, of course, know this and they have a range of strategies to try to draw their texts to our attention. One of these, much employed in the context of a magazine, is to present fairly detailed information to a prospective reader in a similar form to the editorial content in the rest of the magazine. The hope is that readers may be reading magazines in a particular way (usually skimming with occasional bursts of more intensive reading when something catches their interest) and may read the advertisement in the same way, almost before they notice it is not actually editorial matter.

The major difficulty of this text for readers is, therefore, in approaching it sufficiently aware of its purpose that they read it critically, as befits a text which is essentially propaganda.

Text C

The railway timetable makes heavy demands on the previous knowledge of its readers. Although the abbreviations and symbols it employs are explained elsewhere in the full timetable, readers who already know them will have a much easier time of making sense of this text. We need at least to know that symbols such as the E, D and A at the head of three of the columns are important conveyors of meaning (in fact they give information about the dates of operation of the particular services.) Not recognising this could lead to disastrous results, such as arriving at Newton Abbot station at a quarter to midnight to discover that the last Plymouth train actually left at 11.25 pm! Most people have had experiences of not quite reading railway timetables accurately with inconvenient results!

Our approach to reading texts like this is, of course, quite distinctive. Nobody will read every word in a railway timetable, from top to bottom and left to right. That would be a ridiculous way to proceed. Instead we adopt a scanning approach, moving our eyes rapidly over the text until we spot the detail for which we are searching. Most of us are actually very good at this. We get constant practice as we move around our print-saturated world engaging fleetingly with texts such as:

- The signs on the motorway which tell us where to exit
- The shop signs which tell us where to go to buy particular items
- The words on the page of the newspaper which tell us where to find today's TV schedules
- The features of an envelope enclosure which tell us this is just junk mail, etc.

The difficulties the text might cause us are related directly to the code of symbols which it uses and which are unique to this context. Some people may also find confusing the fact that this text actually has to be read from top to bottom rather than the more usual left to right.

PROCESS OR PROCESSES?

You have probably realised from the above activity that the process you went through in reading each of the three texts you were given was slightly different. For each text you drew upon slightly different knowledge and skills. For other texts you might read, your reading process would again be slightly different each time. Think about reading a novel, for example, or a poem. This variation in the reading process depending upon the text read, the purpose for reading and the context in which this reading takes place is very important because it suggests that there is no such thing as the reading process but, in fact, there are many reading processes each with their own subtle differences in emphasis. We will look now, in more detail, at what all these reading processes have in common.

Common elements in reading processes

In reading there are several types of mental activities in which we engage. To look at these activities, consider the following texts:

Text 1

Цан йоу реад тхис?

Text 2

akjhs asjgdjbl opojbeyflqe

Text 3

May cow cat like one only very dog.

Text 4

Furious clouds dream the wet August stamps.

Text 5

Hollis will be fine with that long run.

 ACTIVITY 3.2

You will quickly realise that you cannot actually *read* any of these texts (although with text 5 it will probably seem as if you ought to be able to). What is it about each text which prevents you? Note down for each text what it is that you think stops you being able to read it.

 COMMENTS 3.2

Text 1

In the case of text 1, although you will be able to identify this as something which it might be possible to read, you will probably not be able to do it because you do not recognise the symbols in the text as being in a form which you can respond to. Some of the symbols clearly match symbols which you commonly read, but it is clear from the way they are organised that this is not a text aimed at readers of Roman script languages like English. Your problem is at the level of individual symbols – commonly called *letters*.

Texts 2 and 3

Text 2 is different in that you recognise the symbols, but here they are not organised into groups which you identify as possible to read (*words*). In text 3 the symbols are grouped into words yet you still cannot really read them because the order in which the words occurs does not conform to your idea of recognisable word groupings (*sentences*). The problems with both these texts concern different aspects of what might be termed word and sentence grammar, or syntax.

You may object at this point and say that although the 'sentence' in text 3 does not make sense, you can still 'read' it because you can say each word aloud. This brings us to a question of definition, and, indeed, one of the central areas of controversy in the debate surrounding reading and its teaching. There are those who would argue that being able to say words aloud and recognise these words in one's personal vocabulary does count as reading. Others would argue that reading involves much more than this and requires a response in terms of making sense of extended groups of words. In fact, most modern commentators on reading would now agree that it actually involves both of these aspects – decoding printed symbols into recognisable language *and* constructing meaning through interactions with these symbols. Both are necessary parts of the reading process and neither is sufficient by itself (Adams, 1990).

Text 4

Text 4 seems to be even closer to something we can read. It is recognisably an English sentence so there is no syntactic problem. Yet it would be hard to claim we understood it. Its problem concerns meaning, or semantics. If reading involves the derivation of meaning from printed symbols, then we cannot read this sentence.

Text 5

The problem with text 5 is wider than any of those previously mentioned. Many people will actually feel that they can attribute a meaning to this sentence but the problem is that these meanings will differ from person to person. For some readers, the sentence will tell them that Hollis, a cricketer, will be able to bowl well because he is taking a very long run up. For others, it may convey that Hollis, a dog, will be happy during his stay in the kennels (while his owners are away) because he is in a pen with a large space in which he can exercise. Still others will take the sentence to mean that Hollis, a factory production worker, will now be happy because he is able to concentrate on making the same item for an extended period of time. The difficulty with this sentence is that its meaning is determined by the understanding which a reader *brings to* the text. It emphasises that reading is a transaction between a reader and a text, and the meanings created in one particular act of reading will differ from those created in any other, even of the same text. Thus different people reading the same text are likely to construct different meanings, depending on the knowledge they bring with them, and any individual is likely to construct a slightly different meaning from each reading and re-reading of a particular text.

A MODEL OF THE READING PROCESS

A model which helps to describe what happens when we read is that known as the interactive, or transactional, model (Rumelhart, 1985; Goodman, 1985). This model stresses that the process of reading is a construction of meaning. Diagrammatically it can be represented as in Figure 3.1.

According to this model the reader brings to the act of reading several kinds of knowledge. These are as follows.

Knowledge about how language works

All language speakers have a large fund of implicit knowledge about how language systems work. We have no problem, for example, in completing the following exercises.

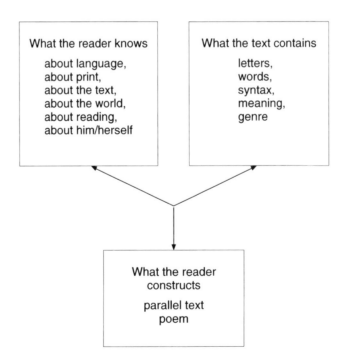

Figure 3.1 An interactive model of reading

- I saw a wug walking down the road. When I looked again it had been joined by another and there were two ––.
- Today I must ruggle my bed. I wish I had ––––– it yesterday.

Our knowledge of language structures enables us to complete these easily, and indeed most children can manage this sort of thing from around the ages of 4 or 5.

Knowledge about print

One of the first things we learn about reading is that it involves paying attention to particular marks on paper. We learn to attend to these black marks (rather than the 'little white rivers' as one child with reading problems thought (Clay, 1972, p. 37)) and we learn how they work, for instance, that they should be followed from left to right and top to bottom.

Knowledge about the text

We usually, when reading, have some prior knowledge about the topic of the text which we can bring to bear to help us make sense of it. We may have previously read some parts of the text, we may have read other texts by the same author or on similar topics. Or we may have chosen the text because it relates to something in which we are interested.

Knowledge about the world

Individuals each have unique profiles of experiences and are each therefore able to bring different world knowledge to their readings. As we saw earlier with the text about Hollis, a person's world knowledge can crucially affect the meanings we attribute to text.

Knowledge about reading

As we gain experience in reading we also develop our understandings about what it involves. There is quite a lot of evidence (for example, Medwell, 1990) that young schoolchildren have fixed in their minds the idea that reading is simply about decoding words and, consequently, that is what they attempt to do when asked to read. As I have been arguing in this Unit, such a belief will get them so far in reading, but it will not get them all the way. A more rounded view will allow us to give attention when we read to gaining meaning *through* attending to the words.

Knowledge about ourselves

We also bring to reading an awareness of ourselves as readers. We may be aware, for instance, that we are careless as readers and, if the text we are reading is particularly important we need to slow down and take more care.

The contribution of the text

Notwithstanding the importance of the knowledge which readers bring to the activity of reading, it could not proceed without a text to read and that text has certain features of which a reader has to be aware. Texts consist of letters grouped into words, grouped in turn into grammatically organised sequences. Texts also have authors who have their own reasons for creating such relatively permanent representations of meaning. Although the author's intended meaning is not the determiner of the meaning created in reading by a reader, it is naturally a powerful influence. Finally, texts are organised differently according to their purposes and this feature is usually known as *text genre*.

The reader's construction

In the act of reading, the reader combines all these sources of knowledge with the information contained in the text itself and constructs a meaning. The meaning taken away by the reader consists neither exactly of what he or she brought to the text nor exactly of what the author intended to convey. Rather, the reader constructs a parallel text to that being read. This process is in essence an extremely creative one. It is described well by Louise Rosenblatt, one of the foremost theorists about reading.

> The reader brings to the text his past experience and present personality. Under the magnetism of the ordered symbols of the text, he marshals his resources and crystallises out from the stuff of memory, thought and feeling a new order, a new experience, which he sees as the poem (not necessarily what we think of as a poem, but *any* literary work created by a reader in the process of reading a text).'
>
> (Rosenblatt, 1978, p. 12)

Unit 4

The writing process

INTRODUCTION

Writing often seems a very mysterious process. When we write, somehow or other, ideas which are in our heads, perhaps only in the very vaguest of forms, have to be shaped into coherent representations in language and transferred onto paper, screen or other media so they can be inspected by some other person. Although we vary greatly in the amount of writing that we do, we all have a tendency to take the process for granted. Even those who write a great deal will, when asked to describe the difficulties of writing, tend to focus upon the original development of ideas rather than on the process of shaping these into language. The term we use to describe having difficulties in writing, 'writer's block', is understood by most people to mean having difficulty in getting ideas for writing rather than difficulty in transferring these to the page.

Yet the process of writing is not so simple. How exactly do we shape our ideas into writeable forms, and does the process then simply involve the transferring of these ideas to a page? Do we all follow the same process in writing or does the process vary according to how skilful we are at writing, how experienced we are, our individual styles or personalities, or any other dimension?

We will begin a closer look at these questions by examining our own writing processes.

 ACTIVITY 4.1

Think about the most recent piece of sustained writing you have done. Examples you might choose could range from a personal letter to a friend to a policy document for your school. How did you actually set about this writing? Jot down, in note form, as much as you can remember about your approach to this task.

It would be very useful if you could compare your approach to this writing task to that of someone else. Are there similarities or differences in the ways you both tackled the task? If there are differences, how might you account for these? Are they merely the result of you both engaging in slightly different writing tasks or are there more fundamental reasons for the differences?

On the basis of your investigations in this activity, try to write down a brief description of what you now consider the process of writing to consist of? (See Suggestions for Answers at the end of this Unit.)

DIMENSIONS OF THE WRITING PROCESS

Our look above at the activities of an adult writer reveals the multiple dimensions involved in the writing process. Let us consider more closely these dimensions.

In order to communicate ideas the writer must compose. This involves:

- Getting and evaluating information
- Evolving and synthesising ideas
- Shaping information and ideas into a form that can be expressed in writing

This is essentially a creative act involving the moulding of ideas and the creation and ordering of knowledge. Composition is, therefore, a learning activity in its own right rather than simply a way of presenting pre-formed ideas. This view of composition, and writing in general, puts emphasis on the role of language as a means of making sense of the world, a view commonly expressed by modern theorists of and researchers into the development of language processes (for example, Wells, 1987).

The writer must also transcribe the composition. This involves choosing an appropriate form and presenting a correct layout. Transcription also sometimes requires attention to accuracy in spelling, grammar, punctuation and handwriting. It is clear that transcription assumes different levels of importance depending upon the purpose of and audience for a piece of writing. A letter to a bank manager or an application for a job require much more care to be given to features such as spelling and handwriting than do a shopping list or the notes we may take during a lecture. Yet transcription always takes place and always demands some of our attention in writing.

Ideally, the writer should be able to co-ordinate these two dimensions of writing, but this is often not the case. Composition and transcription may inhibit one another and orchestrating the two may be very difficult. Many adults find that they make more mistakes and changes when writing something important because their minds are so involved with composing the ideas. For children, who may have less than complete mastery of the processes involved, this co-ordination is doubly difficult.

The result of this problem of co-ordination is sometimes that children come to believe that particular parts of the writing process are more important than others and should take the lion's share of their attention. Most teachers are well aware of this – a fact which should enable you to complete the following activity easily.

a ACTIVITY 4.2

As part of a study of children's ideas about writing in school, a large group of primary children, from 7 to 11 years old, were asked to write a response to the following statement:

Someone in the class below yours has asked you what the writing will be like when he/she comes into your class. Write and tell him/her, and try to give him/her some useful advice about what he/she will have to do to do good writing in your class.

The children's responses were read and a record kept of their mentions of particular aspects of writing. The following aspects were mentioned:

- Characters
- Ideas
- Length
- Layout
- Neatness
- Punctuation
- Spelling
- Structure
- Style
- Tools
- Words

1   Can you make a prediction about the order of popularity of each of these aspects, in terms of the number of times they were mentioned by the children? (Answers at the end of this Unit.)
2   You might ask children in your own class to respond to the statement above and compare their responses with those described below.

INTRODUCING THE WRITING PROCESS

One way of overcoming the problem of orchestrating dimensions of writing is to approach composition and transcription separately with children. This might be done by introducing them to the drafting process, that is, to the idea that a piece of writing may go through several versions. This approach can allow the writer the freedom to concentrate firstly on composition, and then later to deal with transcription. Drafting, however, implies more than just 'writing it in rough first'. It allows children to get to grips with three very important processes in writing: planning, revision and editing (Graves, 1983).

Planning

Many children have only vague notions about planning. Elizabeth (8 years old), when asked how she plans her writing, said, 'I write the first idea, then I get another one and I write it down, and I go on until I've run out, and that's the end.' While this may be appropriate in a few situations, it is not the way adult writers work, nor is it the ideal way for children to work. Planning can help children to generate ideas and formulate thoughts. Noting down their plans for writing can also help children remember all the ideas they want to work with. Eira (7 years old) commented, 'The plan sort of helps when it brings back the ideas I forget, and I get new ones then too.' If the burden of memory is alleviated, then the child may be better able to reflect upon and organise those ideas.

 ACTIVITY 4.3

It would be useful at this point for you to note down a few thoughts about how you might introduce ideas and strategies for planning writing to your class. This activity would be even better done as a whole-school staff and ideas shared between colleagues.

There are many ways to plan a piece of writing: a child may jot down a few key words from a class brainstorming session, they may create idea webs, or there may be a class 'formula' introduced by the teacher.

- One teacher introduced her class of 9 year olds to the idea of topic webs. They began with the topic for writing in the centre and then brainstormed connected ideas which were added to the web. This teacher taught her children that 'Ideas are like butterflies; if you don't catch them quickly and write them down, they soon flutter away.'
- Another teacher decided to introduce her class of 7 year olds to planning by asking them to draw 'beginning', 'middle', and 'end' boxes and put key words into them. This focused their attention on the structure of their writing.
- Another idea which has been successfully used by teachers is to give children frameworks around which to structure their writing (see Lewis and Wray, 1995 for more details of this approach). Writing frames provide children with sets of sentence starts and connectives into which they work their own ideas. The frame helps keep their writing coherent and can act as a plan and a set of prompts to writing.

Different frames can help children plan different types of writing. If, for example, they are reporting on research they have been carrying out using information books, they may use a frame like the following:

Although I already knew that

I have learnt some new facts. I learnt that

I also learnt that

Another fact I learnt

However the most interesting thing I learnt was

If, however, they are planning to write an argument in favour of a particular viewpoint, the frame may look like this:

Although not every body would agree, I want to argue that

I have several reasons for arguing for this point of view. My first reason is

A further reason is

Furthermore

Therefore, although some people argue that

I think I have shown that

Many children will need this sort of help to get started, but it is important that through their school careers they experience planning in different ways, for two main reasons. Firstly, some types of planning, like the examples above, help develop certain features only of writing. More importantly, though, teachers are aiming to give children sufficient experience to enable them to choose a form of planning most suited to their needs. The form and amount of planning necessary depends on the child and on the task.

Revision

If children are allowed to draft work they are more likely to see it as provisional, and therefore change and improve it (Wray, 1990). Children, and adults, may need to reflect upon and revise their compositions several times.

It is important to realise the difference between revision and editing. Revision implies qualitative changes of content, style or sequence. Although it is the most difficult aspect of the writing process to introduce, revision of drafted writing should naturally follow on from planning. The questions writers ask themselves during revision will depend on the piece of writing, but will include:

- Does it say what I want to say?
- Is it in the right order?
- Is the form right?

ACTIVITY 4.4

Again, it would be useful at this point for you to note down a few ideas about how you might introduce ideas and strategies for revising to your class. This activity would be even better done as a whole-school staff and ideas shared between colleagues.

Many teachers offer their children sets of questions to get them started, such as:

- Does everything make sense?
- Could I add something?
- Should I leave anything out?
- Are there any parts in the wrong order?

These questions can be displayed as posters or cards and children can use them independently, or with a friend. They may be the first step towards enabling children to look critically at their work without the prompting of the teacher.

Revision may involve minor adjustments, like insertions, crossing out etc. or it may necessitate rewriting and moving blocks. Some of these strategies are more difficult than others and it is likely that children will need a great deal of support from their teachers before they are able to use them independently. There are particular techniques to which they can be introduced, such as the use of scissors to physically cut out sections to resequence writing. They may also be fairly resistant to alterations which involve crossing out sections of writing (perhaps because crossings out are often associated in children's minds with mistakes), and will need special reassurance that this kind of revision is approved of by their teachers.

Revising one's own writing can be quite difficult, even for adults. Writers are often too close to their own writing to be able to look at it with a properly critical eye. Because of this, it can often be useful to encourage children to work in small groups to help revise each others' writing. Fresh eyes can spot problems and also help the writer become more able to see these.

Editing

When the writing is at a stage where the author is starting to think about a final draft then editing becomes necessary. Editing involves correcting the surface features of the text: spelling, grammar, punctuation etc. Most children are familiar with this in the form of a teacher's 'marking'. Some teachers mark these surface features automatically, and so children set great store by them. This at least means that editing is the easiest part of the process to introduce. These features of language are important, and although the teacher could correct them quickly and accurately, it is preferable for children to correct work themselves. This is not only a step towards independence, it also allows children to develop transferable strategies for future work.

To support the children in doing this some teachers supply wallcharts and cards offering questions and advice. Such wallcharts may even introduce children to professional proof-readers' codes and children usually enjoy using these. These charts can be used by individuals, or more often, pairs of children. Peer editing is helpful in that it offers the child support, advice and opinions, which can be accepted or rejected depending on the author's judgement. It is also allows realistic organisation of teacher time as purposeful, task-oriented discussion can take place without the teacher's presence (Wray and Gallimore, 1986).

Publication and evaluation

Drafting is a very powerful process that allows children to concentrate separately on the various elements of writing. The emphasis is on producing a better quality product for an audience. This means, of course, that children need to publish and evaluate their writing. In this context publish means simply 'to make public', and this can take many forms. Some work may be read out to a teacher, friend, group or class, perhaps in a designated 'sharing time'. Publication could also mean displaying work so that it becomes reading material in a real sense, from a single piece of writing on the wall to a book written for younger children by a group. In all cases it is important that publication should have the appropriate form and that final decisions about content and so on should be made by the author. When the publication reaches its intended audience then any sort of response can be used for evaluation. This may be between the child and teacher, among a small group, or more widely. In any case, both teachers and children will have to understand the need for constructive criticism.

When publication is the perceived end-point of the writing children are helped to develop their awareness of audience. This has an effect upon both the composition and transcription processes which children need to begin to take account of early in their writing experience. They need, in general, to have experience of writing for a range of purposes.

POSTSCRIPT: THE REFLECTIVE PROCESS

It is important to realise that the description of the process of writing around which this Unit has been structured is still an oversimplification of the true picture. In thinking about your own writing earlier, it probably occurred to you that you do not, for example, think through the whole of your writing before you set pen to paper. Thinking about what to write and transcribing it often take place at the same time. Often, indeed, you may not know exactly what you will write until you have begun to write it. It is fairly easy to think of occasions when this has happened.

The process of writing is not linear in operation in the sense of a series of steps through which writers proceed in order. Rather, the process is recursive and reflective with several parts operating simultaneously.

This has several implications for the teaching of writing which you might consider. How might you allow for these things in your teaching?

1   Children need time to reflect upon their writing.
2   Allowance needs to be given for the erratic nature of the process.
3   Children might benefit from discussing their approaches to writing with their classmates.

SUGGESTIONS FOR ANSWERS

Activity 4.1

You probably discerned several stages to the process of writing. The sequence below may not agree completely with your own description but might be useful as a starting point for discussion.

In order to produce a piece of writing, the writer needs to:

- Have something worth saying
- Decide that writing is the most appropriate medium for saying this
- Have an audience in mind for what will be written
- Think about how ideas will be expressed
- Put these expressions down on paper
- Reconsider what has been written, and perhaps make alterations
- Pass on the writing to where it was intended to go

These stages do not include the pencil sharpening, false starts, coffee making and various other activities that some writers find essential! Very few adults are able to produce a neat, accurate piece of writing that says all that they want to say in the appropriate style and form at one short sitting. Interruptions and disruptions are normal in experiences of writing rather than exceptions.

Activity 4.2

The results of the survey were as follows:

- *Spelling* (mentioned 579 times, that is, 19.88 per cent of the total number of mentions of all features). It would usually be referred to by phrases such as, 'Make sure you get your spellings right', or 'Use a dictionary to spell words you don't know.'
- *Neatness* (503 – 17.27 per cent). This would be referred to by statements like, 'Do your best handwriting' or 'Make sure it is not messy.'
- *Length* (372 – 12.77 per cent). Many children stressed that the writing had to be 'long enough', although a significant number warned not to make it too long 'because Miss might get bored'.
- *Ideas* (359 – 12.33 per cent). There were several comments along the lines of: 'Try to have some funny bits,' or 'Stories should be interesting and exciting.'
- *Punctuation* (312 – 10.71 per cent). Here were mentions of the need for full stops and capital letters, commas and speech marks.

- *Words* (213 – 7.31 per cent). Statements were used such as 'Don't use the same word over and over again.'
- *Tools* (160 – 5.49 per cent). There was surprisingly frequent mention of the materials with which to write, such as 'make sure your pencil is sharp', or 'Mr Ellis gets cross if you do not use a ruler to underline the title.'
- *Structure* (132 – 4.53 per cent). There was some mention of structural features such as 'A story needs a beginning, a middle and an end.'
- *Characters* (100 – 3.43 per cent). Some children gave advice such as 'Write about interesting people.'
- *Style* (60 – 2.06 per cent). Relatively few mentions were made of stylistic features such as 'In poems you can repeat words to make it sound good', or 'Don't begin sentences with "and".'
- *Layout* (46 – 1.58 per cent). Some children made references to the drawing of a margin or the placing of the date etc.

(Further details of this research study can be found in Wray, 1994).

A typical piece of writing in the survey was John's, who wrote:

frist you put your pencle down and coppey a letter what someone put down like you are darwing make your big letters go up to the line above. put capitals letters at the bigan of centens and full stop at the end. get on with your work. if you doing story's don't let it cary on to long. don't make to much smches and used rubbers to much do your comers and speach mark's do your marging and don't wander about.

It seems that primary children on the whole do not value aspects of writing connected with composition but pay greater attention to transcription. This suggests that when children are writing they are likely to be giving so much attention to transcribing that they have little to spare for composition, which is arguably the most important dimension of writing. To develop fully as writers children will need help in orchestrating the dimensions.

Writing can be an individual . . .

. . . or a collaborative process.

The purposes and processes of talk

INTRODUCTION

Talk is such a universal activity that we rarely consider what it does for us. It is very revealing to try to analyse the purposes of this taken-for-granted activity. Such an analysis can provide us with a 'map' of the uses of talk against which we can compare the ways in which talk is typically used in classrooms. In this Unit we shall look firstly at a range of purposes for talk and then go on to examine the potential and predominant patterns of talk in primary classrooms.

WHAT DOES TALK DO FOR US?

The common-sense answer to the question of what talk does for us is that it is mainly a medium for communication with other people. Talk is seen largely as a vehicle for the passing of ideas from one person to another. Of course, this is an important function of talk but if we see it as only, or even mainly, serving this purpose, we risk ignoring several other important functions which it serves. To illustrate this point, let us look at a few examples of talk in action. In each of the following examples, what purpose is the talk serving?

Example 1

Two women walk past each other on a busy street. The following conversation ensues:

Hello. It's lovely to see you. How are you?
Oh, I'm fine, thanks. How are you?

Fine, thanks. How're the family?
They're OK. How's John?
Oh, busy as ever. But he's fine really.
Good. Anyway, must rush. I want to get to the bank before it closes. Give us a ring and we'll
    get together sometime.
Yes, that'd be good. Bye for now.
Bye.

Example 2

A man is trying to get a lawn mower to work so that he can mow his lawn. He is talking
as he does so.

Now, come on, work, you useless machine. God, why are you always so difficult? Work! ...
    That's better. Now just you carry on.

Example 3

A teacher is having a conversation with a group of infant children about the birds which
have made a nest in the guttering surrounding their classroom.

Teacher: What did we see yesterday?
Pupil: All their heads popped up. And they all made a noise. And they all went ... and two
    went down. No. One went down and ... they both they stayed up ... And for a little while
    they both popped down again.

In each of these examples some communication has taken place (although in Example 2 we
might have to sustain the notion of an 'intelligent lawnmower' in order to see this as
communication!) But it is also clear that in each example something else is going on.

Example 1

In Example 1 there are questions to be asked about what actually has been communicated.
Much of this exchange is ritualised and the two speakers probably gave little thought to the
content of what they each said. The main function of their talk was probably not to
communicate anything in particular, but simply to interact socially. This social interactive
function of talk is a good deal more common than we might think and it usually operates
in parallel to the communicative function. We regularly use phrases in conversation such
as, 'you know', 'Really? Well I never!' and so on, which carry little message but do act to
maintain the social relationship between speakers.

Example 2

In Example 2 the communicative function of talk is less salient. Instead, the talk here is serving the function of emotional expression. Talk is universally used in this way, even if sometimes 'under the breath', to 'let off steam'. This expressive function is seen equally in conversation. There are many ways open to speakers to express what they want to say and so the exact phrasing they choose almost inevitably reflects elements of their feelings towards what they are talking about. For instance, I might, in different conversations, refer to my computer as 'this infernal machine' or 'this wizard box of tricks', each of which reveals a different part of my ambivalent feelings towards it.

Example 3

In Example 3 there clearly is some communication, with information passed between the speakers in answer to a direct question. But something else is happening here as well. The child's speech suggests that he is using talk to clarify his thoughts about the event he is describing. His talk here is typical of informal conversation in which we often introduce ideas without previously thinking them through and in fact use speech as a means of thinking things out. This characteristic of talk is a very powerful feature which can completely change our view of learning. It suggests that talking about something is a way of learning about it. Learning has been seen as the expansion and modification of existing ways of conceiving the world in the light of alternative ways, with the learner actively constructing his/her own models of reality (Bruner and Haste, 1987). If learning is seen in this way then the importance of talking as the chief medium for working out these constructions becomes clear. In the view of the learner as an active constructor of knowledge (rather than a passive receiver), talk has the place of a medium, probably the most powerful medium, for pushing forward new interpretations, debating their implications, trying out possibilities and linking new ideas with those previously held.

This process can be seen at work in many situations. It occurs when we discuss issues with other people. We rarely come to these discussions with our ideas fully formed and rehearsed. Instead, we take note of what others say and reshape our ideas in the light of others' contributions. To discuss is to think, and through the effort of 'thinking on our feet' we develop our ideas. In other words, we learn. The process also occurs when we teach. Many teachers will testify that the first time they really understood some things was when they tried to explain them to children. The act of trying to express ideas clarifies them.

TALK IN ACTION

To examine these four functions of talk in action, let us look at the following extract from a classroom conversation (taken from Hughes, 1994). The conversation is between the teacher and a group of children. The group had just visited a wild area which one of them, David, had discovered close to the school playground. They had found some small creatures and brought them back to put them in a tank in the classroom:

1   *Teacher*: I really enjoyed that, didn't you?

2   *Ian*: I did, I really did.

3   *Sarah*: I specially liked all they little baby snails.

4   *David*: I like they things, look, they …

5   *Ian*: Worms

6   *Leanne*: I hates worms … yuk … I hates them all slimy.

7   *Teacher*: Well, they can't help being slimy can they?

8   *Louise*: Why have they got slimy bits? Snakes 'ant got slimy bits like they. When that man came from his zoo with snakes he told us they weren't slimy.

9   *David*: I touched a snake.

10 *Ian*: I touched a frog.

11 *Leanne*: I held the little owl and he pecks me.

12 *Teacher*: Well, why have worms got slimy bits? Louise asked us an interesting question there. Can anyone …?

13 *Richard*: It's because they live in the ground and that can hurt if they not slimy … and snails is slimy when they moves.

14 *David*: Look, I can see all his slimy on the glass.

15 *Kevin*: That silly … drinks in glass.

16 *Sarah*: I'm thirsty.

17 *Louise*: I'm thirsty now.

18 *Teacher*: You can all have a drink in a minute. Let's just … let's just … who can help me to show the children the little snail climbing up the glass tank? Sit down lovie, so that we can see.

19 *Sarah*: Look at the little snail and there's his big mum in the grass.

20 *David*: I can see all the slimy on the glass.

21 *Kevin*: Is it like glue? Not glue like when we do sticking at school.

22 *Sarah*: Not that white sort of glue, like …

23 *Richard*: I did sticking, I made a big card for my Nan.

24 *Teacher*: So you did, but do you think this snail is really stuck with glue?

25 *Peter*: He's not stuck properly, he can still go up.

26 *Ross*: Yeah, he's going right up to the top of the glass.

27 *Richard*: And then he'll fall on the ground and a big bird'll fly in and eat him.

28 *Sarah*: Ah, poor snail … I feel really sorry for poor little creatures being ate.

29 *Richard*: That's what birds do to snails.

30 *Ross*: Then things eat birds and then all things get eaten up.

31 *Richard*: If things don't then they all die.

32 *Teacher*: Well, I don't think a bird will get this snail because he's in the classroom. I think we better take them all back after, don't you?

33 *Sarah*: No, I don't want that little snail to get ate up … I want to keep him.

34 *David*: I want to keep all a they …

35 *Teacher*: Well we can keep them for a little while but we'll have to find them food.

36 *David*: Snails eat grass and leaves and things like that don't they?

ACTIVITY 5.1

In the extract above, try to find some examples of each of the four functions of talk which have been discussed.

1   When is talk used to communicate, that is, pass information between one person and another?
2   When is talk used for the maintenance of social relationships?
3   When is talk used to express feelings?
4   When is talk used to work out and explore ideas?

COMMENTS 5.1

Here are just a few of the instances you might have pointed to. One of the most fascinating things about transcripts of discussion, especially it seems, classroom discussion, is their richness in terms of source material for analysis. There are many more things to notice in this extract than can possibly be mentioned in the space available here.

Communication

The extract is full of the participants telling each other things. The children tell each other what they liked about the visit (3, 4, 5), what they did during the visit (9, 10, 11), what they can see at the moment (14, 19, 20, 26) and what they know about the small creatures they are examining (13, 27, 29, 30, 31, 36).

Perhaps because of the open-ended nature of this discussion, the person who communicates least is, in fact, the teacher. This might be a little surprising as it is likely that she knows more about the creatures under examination than any of the other participants. Why do you think the teacher does not use her talk here to pass on information?

It is also of interest that in the teacher's seven contributions to this discussion, she asks seven questions. We discuss this feature of teacher classroom talk elsewhere in the Unit, but you might at this point want to speculate on why questions dominate this teacher's contributions.

Social interaction

The social interaction in this extract is shown most of all in the way all the participants respond to each other's contributions. These children have clearly learnt a crucial aspect of discussion, that is, taking turns and building up a conversation. There is some evidence that young children learn to engage in turn-taking conversations in this way some time before they actually learn to speak. This fits a view of language acquisition which argues that language exists to satisfy social needs first and foremost.

There are also examples in this discussion of participants using language to create joint attention. For example, the teacher's 'didn't you?' in (1) and David's 'Look' in (14).

Expression of feelings

There are lots of examples of expressive talk here. These children clearly feel fairly strongly about the animals they are examining and show it as, for example, in Leanne's 'Yuk' (6) and Sarah's 'poor snail' (28).

Working out ideas

There are several instances in this extract which suggest some working out of ideas on the parts of the participants. Firstly, the children are quite prepared to offer up their tentative ideas for acceptance, elaboration or rejection by the rest of the group. Louise (8), for example, tries to work out why the worms are slimy which inspires other members of the group to share their experiences of other animals. Richard eventually gives an answer after the teacher refocuses the question. Similarly, Kevin (21) tries to find something with which to compare the 'the slimy' and again sparks off an elaboration by other children. Exchanges like these are typical of discussion and give positive evidence of the value of group working in a school context. In terms of the learning of the group, the whole is definitely greater than the sum of the parts.

A second kind of talk which these children use a lot is very important to their learning yet can often be disregarded or dismissed by teachers. Good examples of this are seen in Richard's remark about 'sticking' (23) and the short sequence of experiences related by David, Ian and Leanne (9, 10, 11). Such comments can often seem to teachers to be simple red herrings and distractions to the main theme of the conversation. They respond (as this teacher does) by trying to get the children back onto the point. This 'talking at a tangent' can, however, be itself seen as a learning process. If learning is defined as 'the expansion and modification of existing ways of conceiving the world in the light of alternative ways' (Wray and Medwell, 1994) then a crucial element in learning is the linking of new experiences with previously held ideas. Anecdotes which are sparked off by new ideas represent precisely the places where this linking is taking place. The talker, by telling a personal anecdote, is showing where his or her personal links are. Learning is an idiosyncratic process; different learners make the links in different ways and at different points. It is difficult, therefore, for teachers to be aware of the learning needs of individuals unless they listen carefully to the anecdotes which new ideas set off.

We have looked here at only a very brief extract of classroom discussion. The processes referred to happen all the time in discussion and all have implications for learning. Together they suggest that teachers need to give very careful consideration to the place of talk in their classrooms.

 ACTIVITY 5.2

Tape record a group of children engaged in a discussion about a topic which interests them. This does not have to be a topic set by a teacher. It would be better, and probably result in more natural talk, if you were not actually present at the discussion, but simply eavesdropped by means of the tape recorder.

Listen to the recording and try to identify elements which suggest learning on the part of the speakers. Make a note of these and, if possible, share them with a colleague.

TALK IN CLASSROOMS

In the next section of this unit we shall examine the current state of classroom talk using evidence from research and from your own investigations. How conducive an environment are classrooms for the rich purposes of talk that we have outlined above?

The most obvious characteristic of talk inside classrooms is that it is different from that which takes place outside school. Teachers often feel this very keenly and 'teacher talk' has proved to be ripe ground for satire. While Joyce Grenfell's speaking style is clearly an exaggeration, it does contain sufficient truth to embarrass many teacher listeners.

Children, likewise, tend not to talk in classrooms in the same way as they do outside. In the classroom they may be required to produce a more completed style of speech ('answer with a complete sentence'), and they will almost certainly spend much of their talking time answering questions. Some studies have suggested that from two thirds to three-quarters of children's talk in classrooms consists of them giving answers to questions posed by their teachers.

For both children and teachers, talking in classrooms is an activity which appears to be governed by sets of rules. Of course, it is unlikely that any of the participants in the 'language game of teaching' (Bellack *et al.*, 1966) could explicitly describe what the rules are, just as no user of language can fully describe the grammatical rules of that language. The important fact is, though, that participants act as if they knew the rules. It is rare for users of language, or talkers in classrooms, to break the rules of that activity.

So what are the rules of classroom talk?

 ACTIVITY 5.3

Try to list some of the rules about talking which apply in your classroom. Some of the questions you might ask include:

- What restrictions do you place upon children talking?
- Are there times and places when these restrictions are relaxed?
- Do you operate a system by which children ask for and receive permission to talk?
- Are there any kinds of talk you will not accept from children?

TALK RULES

Evidence from many studies (see Edwards and Westgate, 1987, for a thorough review) suggests that the rules of classroom talk are, by and large, universal, although they vary in the rigidity with which they are enforced. They consist of rules about the context of talk and rules about its content.

In terms of context, the following things seem generally to be true (Sinclair and Coulthard, 1975):

1   Teachers decide who will speak and for how long.
2   Teachers plan and run the system by which those who wish to speak can have the opportunity to do so. This is usually the 'hands-up' system, although teachers have the power to bypass this, for instance by asking children without their hands up.
3   Teachers have the final say over the acceptability of particular contributions. They can indicate their approval, or lack of it, verbally or non-verbally.
4   Teachers can alter any of the rules at their discretion. They may, for instance, allow greater freedom of talking in certain lessons (e.g. Art), or on certain occasions (e.g. discussion times).

The rules about the content of talk can be inferred from an examination of the salient features of classroom talk. We shall do this by looking closely at an extract from a History lesson with a class of 8 to 9 year olds. The teacher introduces the lesson.

1   *Teacher*: Now, I want you put your books away and listen carefully. We're going to talk about the ships the Vikings used. Put your book away, Rosie. That's a good girl. Right. Now, do you remember, last week we looked at some slides about the Vikings and some of the slides showed us pictures of their ships? Can anyone remember anything we said about their ships? Paul, I'm talking. Anyone remember anything we talked about?
2   *P1*: They had shields on them.
3   *Teacher*: Yes, good. They had shields on them. Where were the shields?
4   *P1*: On the sides.
5   *Teacher*: On the sides of …?
6   *P1*: The boats.
7   *Teacher*: The sides of the boats, yes. Why do you think they had shields on the sides of their ships? Stephen?
8   *P2*: To stop arrows, Miss.

9   *Teacher*: Well, yes, they might have been to stop arrows. Can anyone think of another reason? … Paul, well if you listened and stopped fiddling with your pencil, you might understand better … Any other reasons? … Yes, Lisa?

10 *P3*: So nobody could kill them, Miss?

11 *Teacher*: Well, yes, that's the same as Stephen's, isn't it? So nobody could shoot arrows at them and kill them. But I think there was another reason too. You just think if you were Vikings, all of you packed tightly on board those little ships. And you've not got much room for anything on board but you've got these big shields. What do you think you might do with them to get them out of the way? … Where might you put them?

12 *P4*: Hang them up.

13 *Teacher*: Yes, good, you'd hang them outside your ship so they wouldn't be in the way, wouldn't you? Now, what else do you remember about the Vikings' ships? … Yes, dear, I'm sure it'll be all right if you leave it alone … What about their shape?

14 *P5*: They had dragons on, Miss.

15 *Teacher*: Dragons. Tell me more about the dragons, Paul.

16 *P5*: They had dragons on the front of the ships, like big sea monsters, so the ships looked like sea monsters.

17 *Teacher*: Yes, very good, they would carve the fronts of their ships to look like sea monsters. Do you remember, we saw some pictures of an old Viking ship that was found and that had a sea monster's head on it. Do you remember that ship, what shape was it? Was it round and wide, or long and narrow? What shape was it?

18 *P3*: It was long and narrow, Miss.

19 *Teacher*: Good, Lisa. It was long and narrow. Now I wonder why it was that shape. Why wasn't it wide and round, I wonder? … Anyone?

20 *P6*: … carrying things.

21 *Teacher*: Sorry, Gary, carrying things?

22 *P6*: Carrying lots of things, like axes and swords and horses. Had to have lots of room.

23 *Teacher*: Yes, they needed lots of room. But why was the ship long and thin, … Rosie?

24 *P7*: I saw a ship in my book, Miss, and that was big and wide. It had lots of men on board and guns and things so it had to be wide or it would have rolled over, Miss.

25 *Teacher*: Well, I don't think that was a Viking ship, was it Rosie? Their ships were long and narrow. They wanted them to go as fast as possible so they had to make them narrow. You know, it's like the canoes that people use in races. They want to go fast so they have their canoes as narrow as they can. They wouldn't go fast in a wide canoe, would they?

26 *P7*: My brother went on a canoe, Miss, with his school. But he fell in.

27 *Teacher*: Oh dear, Rosie, I hope he was all right. Now, what about the Viking ships, what kind of sails did they have?

ACTIVITY 5.4

Before reading any further it would be useful for you to jot down your impressions of this extract of classroom talk and the likely learning which may be taking place. (See Suggestions for Answers at the end of this Unit.)

COMMENTS 5.4

The pattern of discourse we see in this extract is found in classrooms from infant schools to sixth forms. It has been given various names such as Solicitation – Response – Reaction (Bellack *et al.*, 1966), or Initiation – Response – Feedback (Sinclair and Coulthard, 1975), or, because of its characteristic to-and-fro nature 'verbal ping-pong'. The cycle consists of three 'moves', typically:

1   The teacher asks a question.
2   A pupil volunteers an answer.
3   The teacher evaluates that answer.

Because in every cycle of discourse the teacher speaks twice for each child utterance, it provides a good explanation for another well-documented finding: the so-called two-thirds rule (Flanders, 1970). This rule states that:

- Two-thirds of classroom talk is done by the teacher.
- Two-thirds of this talk consists of asking questions.

This rule could be extended by a further statement, well illustrated in this extract:

- Two-thirds of teacher questions demand only recall.

The fact that all the teacher's questions in this extract are of this kind suggests a particular view of learning. According to this view children, to learn a body of material, have to be taken through it in an orderly sequence (determined by the teacher, who already knows the material). They are 'taught' by a combination of lecturing and questioning which draws them through the desired sequence. The answers they give to the teacher's questions indicate whether or not they are 'following' the lesson. This approach to teaching and learning has been given the name 'transmission' because of its underlying view that knowledge resides outside of children and has to be transmitted inside them by the teacher. Because this knowledge is held to be an objective entity it should be transmitted in as unaltered a state as possible, feedback on which is provided by children's answers to questions (Barnes, 1976).

This view of learning contradicts that generally held by modern theorists and researchers. If we conceive of learners as active constructors of their own knowledge, engaging in what Gordon Wells calls 'the guided reinvention of knowledge' (Wells, 1987), we see the unlikelihood of learning proceeding through the wholesale adoption of constructions of knowledge which have been formulated by other people. Learners have to make sense of knowledge for themselves, and to do this they need the opportunity to explore, interpret, and come to terms with new information. Transmission teaching does not provide these opportunities, because it has a completely different view of the role of children's talk.

 ACTIVITY 5.5

Tape record one of your own class lessons and try to analyse the talk within it in a similar way to the above analysis.

Do you see evidence of the Initiation–Response–Feedback discourse structure?

What scope is there in your lesson for the children to use their talk to make their own sense of the ideas and information with which they are dealing?

TRANSFORMING TALK

You might feel that the analysis of classroom talk put forward so far in this Unit is a little hard on teachers. It is certainly true that many teachers realise very well the potential in terms of children's learning of engaging them in active open-ended discussion about topics of interest. Yet transmission models of teaching seem all too prevalent, at all phases of education. Why should this be?

According to Edwards and Westgate (1987), there are three main reasons for the prevalence of transmission-style class discussion.

- Teachers' lack of understanding of the role of talk in the learning process. If teachers are not convinced that talk can be a key factor in children's learning, they will not make sufficient provision for it in their classrooms.
- The pressurised nature of the curriculum, with teachers perceiving their task as to 'get through' large bodies of content with their classes. Allowing children scope to explore ideas and make their own connections, however desirable in terms of quality of learning, conflicts with the demands of this curriculum.
- Large class sizes. Even if teachers are convinced of the importance of children's talk to their learning and prepared to stress quality of learning against quantity, they may still have simply too many children to deal with at once to make it a feasible way to organise their work.

Because, for whatever reason, it is extremely difficult to allow sufficient space for children's exploratory talk in busy classrooms, a teacher keen to involve children in this will almost certainly make use of some form of group activities. There are certainly plenty of benefits to be gained from group talk, that is, talk between a small group of children who are working together to solve a joint problem or make joint decisions (Wade, 1985).

Engaging in this kind of group talk can give children the opportunity, first of all, to express tentative ideas and explore them in a sympathetic context. Because the group are working together and not competing for scarce speaking rights, there is less pressure on them to express only fully worked through ideas. They have the chance to put forward tentative ideas for others in the group to support, modify or argue with. Several things follow from this. In this context children are collaborating with others rather than competing against them. Much of children's school experience will emphasise competition at the expense of co-operation, and many children, in fact, find it difficult to collaborate. Yet modern society requires citizens who can work as teams. Group work is the first step towards this.

In the context of group talk children are forced to justify their opinions and ideas, which encourages greater reflection upon them. They can also learn to have greater confidence in their own ideas. Most people, even adults, are far more confident about expressing their ideas in front of a small group rather than a large one, especially if that small group has some sympathy with these ideas because they are all working on the same problem.

Although group talk gives children common reference points, it also brings together a range of backgrounds and perspectives. Having to work with people who see things from different points of view, and who may have different cultural backgrounds and experiences can in itself bring about a widening of children's views of the world. It also forces children to take into account the needs of their audience as they express their ideas in talk. Egocentricity can be lessened by the need to take others ideas into consideration and see things from others' points of view.

Finally group talk also places emphasis upon listening as well as talking. To fulfil the task of the group, children have to listen sympathetically and/or critically to the ideas of their peers, and react appropriately to them. This again is practice they probably get too little of, but is vital for successful group work.

Group talk can, therefore, offer one way of increasing the learning productivity of talk in the classroom. It has much to commend it and its potential needs to be explored.

SUGGESTIONS FOR ANSWERS

Activity 5.4

The first point to note is that the teacher dominates the talk. She speaks alternately with the children and her speeches are much longer than theirs. No pupil gets the opportunity to talk for longer than a few seconds, and they only speak when they are invited to do so.

The teacher's talk consists of three types of utterance. She spends quite some time telling the class things. This 'lecturing' occurs mainly in her longest speeches (11), (17) and (25), and functions as an information-adding device to develop the lesson. An alternative strategy she uses to do this is to ask questions. All but one of the teacher's speeches contains at least one question and her 14 contributions to the dialogue contain 24 questions. These questions give the children their only ways into the dialogue, by answering them. Each of the questions is a 'display' question (Wells, 1987); that is, it is asked not because the teacher wants to know the answer, but because she wants to know if the children do.

Her third type of utterance is to repeat the children's answers. This repetition serves the function of evaluating their answers. By repeating the answer she indicates approval of the speaker. When she does not approve of the answer she responds with a 'Well'. It is likely that this class of children know her style well enough by now to recognise the tone of voice she uses for this as a polite rejection of their ideas.

Notice also how this teacher, in contrast to the teacher in the earlier discussion of the small creatures, treats children's anecdotes. In the extract, Rosie twice (24 and 26) tries to bring in experiences which she has been prompted to think of by the discussion of Viking ships. These inserts do not, however, fit with the teacher's plans for the progression of this lesson and she wastes little time in getting back on course.

Unit 6

Looking at literacy in classrooms

INTRODUCTION

It is a truism to say that one of the purposes for the teaching of literacy in school is to enable children to use literacy effectively in their lives outside school. What is not so often considered, however, is that this does not simply mean preparing children for the ways they will use literacy as adults. Children in fact use literacy in the world outside school from a very early stage in their lives, using reading and writing to solve their own problems, meet their own needs and pursue their own interests in a variety of ways. It clearly makes sense if their experiences of literacy inside school fit their perceptions of it as a crucial, socially relevant process out of school.

The purpose of this chapter is to examine how the messages about the uses and the operation of literacy which children might get in a typical primary classroom coincide, or do not, with their knowledge and uses of literacy outside school. The chapter is constructed around a description of a, hopefully, fairly typical lower junior (Year 3/4) classroom. As we examine this classroom in more detail we shall be concentrating particularly on the ways in which the classroom environment, the activities provided, and the actions of the participants in this classroom may influence the beliefs the children come to hold about what literacy is and what it involves. It can be quite difficult to tease out the messages children get from particular elements of their experience of a classroom. Much of this analysis is speculative, and we may decide that children receive contradictory messages from different aspects of their classroom. But it can still be revealing to try to look at a classroom in this rather different way.

We shall concentrate first of all on the classroom itself, especially as a physical and social environment. As we look for the first time think generally about the kinds of literacy experiences provided for the children in this classroom.

- Do you think the children in this classroom are likely to be encouraged to regard literacy activities as worthwhile and as enjoyable?
- What might the classroom environment be conveying to them about the nature of literacy and what counts as literate behaviour?
- How do these messages fit with the literacy demands of the world outside the school?

Make some notes about your reactions to these questions as you read, and compare them with the observations later in the chapter.

The classroom environment

The classroom is reasonably spacious. Although it contains thirty-two children they are not obviously squashed together, and indeed there are parts of the classroom which are empty at the moment. The major furniture in the classroom is a series of rectangular and circular tables arranged in no obvious pattern in the middle of the room. One corner of the room has a rectangular piece of carpet on the floor, with several cushions scattered on it. There are also some chairs here, but no tables. On the walls in this corner are two low-level bookshelves, and a small book display rack. Books are attractively displayed in these, and on the top of the bookshelves there are some small potted plants and vases of flowers. On the walls above and around the shelves there is a display of children's written work and pictures, under the large caption 'Books We Like'.

Another corner of the room has been designated as the class shop. A counter has been made from a table surrounded by painted corrugated cardboard, on which various home-made 'goods' are on display. These are labelled and have each been given a price. Pinned to the cardboard surround of the shop are various notices such as 'Buy your Mars bar here – only 8p', and 'Your local shop – use it or lose it'. Behind the counter is pinned a list of the goods for sale in the shop along with their prices. There is also a toy till and a supply of plastic coins.

In a third corner of the room are two tables upon which are arranged a variety of mathematics equipment such as weighing scales and sets of small wooden cubes. There is a label on the wall above these tables which says 'Maths Corner'. On a shelf next to these tables are some plastic boxes containing a variety of Maths workcards. These are labelled as 'Level 1', 'Level 2' etc. On a table adjacent to this corner is a computer.

The fourth corner of the room is occupied by the teacher's desk. This faces out into the room and on it are two piles of exercise books and a large dictionary. There is also a notebook open in front of the teacher. On the wall behind the desk there is a small piece of pinboard on which are various items such as a timetable, and other documents intended for the teacher's eyes, alongside a chart of the children's names indicating books they have read and are currently reading.

The walls of the classroom are attractively decorated with a variety of displays incorporating both teacher-produced and child-produced materials. In addition to the book display already mentioned there is a display captioned 'Ourselves' which consists largely of graphs of children's hair colours, eye colours, heights etc. There is also a display entitled 'The Iron Man' which consists of children's written work and pictures mounted around a three dimensional robot made of cardboard boxes painted silver. Hanging from the ceiling in this part of the room are lots of small cardboard robots and bat-like creatures, intermingled with pieces of card on which are written words such as 'stupendous', 'horrendous', 'gigantic' etc.

Now we shall look at the activities in which the children are involved. Read the following description of the activities currently taking place in this classroom and then make some notes about what you think these children might be learning about literacy from the nature of these activities.

- Would you say these children are acting in similar ways to literate adults?
- If not, what differences do you think there are?

The children's activities

Groups of children in the classroom are doing different activities. One group is working with Maths workcards in the area labelled 'Maths Corner'. Some of them are measuring each other's handspans, foot lengths etc. Two are sitting at tables writing in their exercise books. Two more are using a set of balance pans and a jar full of beads to weigh objects such as books, shoes etc. Two children are working with the computer and one of these is typing as the other reads from an exercise book.

A second group are involved in a variety of activities in two corners of the classroom. Some of these are using the class shop. Two are behind the counter taking plastic money in exchange for home-made 'goods', while three more pretend to buy items from the shop. The two 'shop assistants' are using calculators to work out their 'customers' bills, while the 'shoppers' have drawn up shopping lists for themselves on pieces of note paper.

In the opposite corner of the classroom six children are using the book collection. Three boys are excitedly turning the pages of one book while pointing at various items and chattering animatedly. Another boy is laying full length on the carpet obviously engrossed in a book he has chosen. Two girls are browsing among the collection of books on display, occasionally taking one down and looking at it more carefully.

A third group of four children are working together at a large table on a collage picture of a circus scene. There is a book on the table near them open at a picture of the circus. The children are talking together but do not actually seem to be looking at the book.

A fourth group are all sitting quietly at their tables writing on banda worksheets. There are at least five different worksheets being used by this group. Three of these children also have reading scheme books open on their tables. Only two of these children are talking to each other, and these two seem to be involved in an animated discussion about the worksheet they are going together.

One child is currently standing beside the teacher at her desk and is reading to her from a reading scheme book.

Now we shall focus on the teacher's actions.

- What do you think her activities as described here might be conveying to the children about the nature of literacy?
- Would you consider these messages to be useful / desirable / complete?
- How do they compare with the messages children might get from observing literate adults outside school?

The teacher's actions

The teacher is sitting behind her desk, facing the class. A girl is standing alongside her reading from a book. Another child is asking her a question about his work. She diverts her attention from the child reading to answer the boy's question. The girl carries on reading. When the girl reaches the end of the page she is reading, the teacher tells her 'Well done', and the girl goes back to her place. The teacher writes something in her notebook, then calls another child to bring his reading book to her.

After three children have been heard reading in this manner, the teacher gets up from her desk and begins to walk from group to group around the class, occasionally asking individual children questions about the work in which they are engaged. At one point she directs the 'shopping' group to return to their tables and assigns them some Maths worksheets to complete.

After her tour of the classroom she returns to her desk and calls another child to come to read to her.

ANALYSING THE CLASSROOM CAMEO

The main focus in this chapter is an examination of the messages the children in this classroom are getting about literacy. As we look at this we shall find that there are several points on which it is very difficult to judge, because we simply do not have enough information. It is equally as important for you to recognise these points as to make judgements on the basis of the information we do have. If you have made notes about your reactions to this classroom description, you might like to re-read them at this point to pick out points on which you feel you really need fuller information.

1 The classroom

We shall begin by examining more closely the literacy environment in this classroom.

ACTIVITY 6.1

- What do you think this classroom environment is telling these children about what literacy involves and how important it is?
- Do you think the classroom reflects the full range of literacy as experienced by normal adults?
- Are there any areas you think are insufficiently reflected?
- What alterations would you like to make to this classroom to reflect what you might consider a fuller view of literacy?
- Do you think that this classroom is likely to encourage children to have positive attitudes to literacy?

Re-read the first section of the cameo, and spend some time thinking about these questions and noting down your ideas before reading any further. The following comments are not intended as complete answers, but rather as points to stimulate further thought.

COMMENTS 6.1

The first and most positive point to make is that reading is obviously valued and encouraged in this classroom. The attractive book corner and the display based on 'The Iron Man' are clearly designed to encourage reading and to interest the children in books and stories. The teacher has obviously taken care with this aspect, making the books look appealing, and making space for the children's reactions to them – which themselves are likely to encourage further reading. She has also used books to stimulate language development. Clearly a great deal of language usage has gone on in response to 'The Iron Man' and a deliberate attempt has been made to extend children's vocabulary, in this case by highlighting 'gigantic' words.

The chief message the children would seem to be getting from this environment is that reading is enjoyable and fun. This is entirely commendable and, of course, the kind of message we would like all classroom environments to convey. It is important, though, to recognise that this is not all there is to literacy. A major function of print in our world is to convey information, and the concept of literacy must include the ability to process this information.

ACTIVITY 6.2

Does this classroom environment assist the children in any way to develop this aspect of literacy? Does it reflect at all the various ways print is used in the world outside school? Spend a few minutes now re-reading the description of this classroom, looking for instances where print is used to convey information and reflect the print environment of the outside world. Look also for any missed opportunities where print could have been used in this way, but is not.

COMMENTS 6.2

Environmental print

You will almost certainly have pin-pointed the class shop as a good example of the use of environmental print. Here print is being shown to the children to have a value in communicating information. Labels on the goods tell them what is for sale, and price tags tell them how much things cost. This is reinforced by a list of goods and prices displayed behind the counter. Print is also being used here in a way often neglected in classrooms, but everywhere seen in the outside world. Advertising and publicity notices form a major part of everybody's day-to-day print experience and they feature in this part of this classroom. Of course, it is possible that some people might object to this feature on the grounds that children are exposed enough outside school to print trying to persuade them to do things, usually to spend money, without bringing this kind of print into the classroom as well. This is a problem, and we do not know enough about this classroom to know whether the teacher is alert to this and has done anything about it. Before reading on, think for a few minutes about how you might overcome this problem, and use advertising and publicity print in your classroom in a positive way.

Advertising

Clearly it is possible to do this in a big way by making advertising the theme for classroom work. A project in which children actually study advertisements ought to have as a result an increase in children's critical appraisal of the publicity they see around them. Such a project might be widened to include a study of the various advertising media, such as television, posters and so on and would fit into a broadened concept of literacy. It has become quite clear that the processes of learning and applying literacy are equally relevant to other media besides straightforward print. The interpretation of messages from visual media can be seen as an example of reading and, as such, can be described in similar ways.

There are two further suggestions about approaches to advertising which operate in a smaller but perhaps more pervasive way. Firstly, it is likely that advertisements are at their most effective when they are perceived almost peripherally. They are designed to be glanced at rather than studied. If we do study them we tend to bring our critical faculties to bear on them much more readily. This suggests that in the classroom an effective way of stimulating children's critical thinking might be to actually discuss with them notices and signs as they are displayed, rather than simply allow them to become 'part of the wallpaper'. Of course, this discussion should include a healthy dose of scepticism on the part of the teacher.

The second suggestion is to consider who produces such publicity notices. Perhaps involving the children themselves in doing this might alert them to the kinds of techniques and 'tricks' they have to use to try to persuade people to do things, and thereby make them more critical of these techniques when they see them.

Other uses for environmental print

Although environmental print is used to effect in the shopping area, there are several other parts of this classroom in which the opportunity seems to have been missed. Take first the book corner. It seems a little strange that advertising notices are used in the shop, but are not used here, where they might have a very positive and worthwhile effect. The major purpose of arranging the book corner in the way it is here is to persuade children to read, and notices such as 'Reading is good for you', 'You're never alone with a book' etc. would seem to have potential in furthering this message in a way which reflects the use of print that the children see outside school. Of course, children themselves could very profitably be involved in the making of such notices.

It is also a little odd that one of the chief places in this classroom where 'print for information' is used is not intended for the children at all. The teacher's notice board might provide a model for a wider use of this kind of print, and the development of the literacy necessary to use it. A class notice board, containing perhaps a timetable, a list of forthcoming events, a school dinner menu etc., and regularly updated by children and teacher, would seem to have a lot of potential here.

 ACTIVITY 6.3

The other aspect to consider is the incorporation into the classroom of the kinds of texts used widely in everyday life. Often classroom texts become a genre all to themselves and, for the children, have little relationship to the kinds of texts they are familiar with outside school. One good example of this is the text which is perhaps the most familiar of all in our social lives, the newspaper. It is a little surprising that a print resource which, outside school, is used by virtually everyone for information, debate, entertainment and publicity, often has little other use in school than as a table cover during painting sessions! Before reading further you might like to take a little time to consider some of the other ways in which the newspaper might be used as a text in primary classrooms. List some possible ideas for ways you might suggest using newspapers with primary children as a means of developing their literacy. (See Suggestions for Answers at the end of this Unit.)

ACTIVITY 6.4

Newspapers are, of course, not the only 'everyday texts' to have a use in the classroom. Try to list some other texts which you feel you might be able to use in positive ways to broaden your children's concepts of the nature and the purposes of literacy. (See Suggestions for Answers at the end of this Unit.)

COMMENTS 6.4

In the classroom we are studying, the effects of the omissions detailed are mitigated by the positive use of environmental print in the class shop, but there is still a risk here that the children's attitudes towards literacy might be shaped in a way often seen in primary schools. Literacy as defined in schools, and literacy as defined in the outside world tend to be two different things, and there is a danger that children perceive them as entirely separate, and hence do not make the connections they should. For children in school, literacy is basically about books. At best, as in this example classroom, it is about lots of varied and interesting books which they are encouraged to choose from and develop enthusiasms for. At worst, it is only about the reading scheme book they are told to read, two pages at a time, out loud to their teacher, every couple of days. For children outside school, literacy is about the many and varied ways print is used to give information, to persuade, to warn, to create and develop relationships, and, above all, to convey meaning. Separation of the two literacies in this way does not necessarily mean that children will fail to learn to cope with print in the everyday world. Most adults, in fact, manage quite well with most of it without being specifically taught. What it does mean, though, is that school may be seen as fairly irrelevant to real literacy, and the kinds of literacy it teaches as peripheral and very specialised to a particular environment.

2 The children's activities

Our next step is to look more closely at what the children are doing in this classroom, and to attempt to analyse the effects these activities may have on their attitudes to literacy.

ACTIVITY 6.5

Remembering our comments about the classroom environment, re-read the section of the cameo which describes the children's activities, and make some brief notes on the kinds of messages about literacy you think are being conveyed to these children by the activities in which they are involved.

- Do these children seem positive towards the literacy activities they are doing?
- Are they involved in the full range of literacy activities?
- If there are areas less fully represented what effects might this be having?
- Do you have any comments about the materials the children are using?
- Are these representative of the range of materials upon which children might exercise their literacy outside school?

COMMENTS 6.5

Sharing experiences

The first point to make about the kinds of activities in which these children are involved is that the teacher's emphasis on encouraging them to enjoy reading books seems to be working well. The group in the book corner are obviously thoroughly enjoying themselves, and one would guess have been convinced that books offer them very worthwhile experiences. They also appear to recognise that reading can be an enjoyable shared experience. In fact, with the exception of one group, the children in this classroom seem quite prepared to co-operate and share their activities, and their use of their reading. Most teachers would agree that this was beneficial for children. Yet it is interesting to note that, as in many classrooms, this co-operation does not seem to extend to reading and language work, where it might be expected to be of major benefit. The reason for this seems to be mostly attributable to the fact that the reading / language group here are following what is basically an individualised scheme of work. Such schemes, typified by reading scheme books linked to sets of worksheets, are extremely popular in many schools. Without doubt, one of the reasons for their popularity is the impression they give of providing a variety of activities matched to the needs of individual children. Hence the schemes are very often used as individualised systems, sometimes in direct contradiction to the advice given by their publishers on how they might be used. This, of course, militates against children discussing and sharing their work, and they begin to pick up the message that literacy activities in school are basically things you do by yourself. Notice that this does not happen as a result of anything the teacher might explicitly state about working together. From the way the rest of this classroom is organised it is likely that the teacher in this example is very receptive to the idea of children working together. It is, rather, a result of the way the reading and language activities themselves are organised. You might consider, at this point, how you might set about developing co-operative work in activities involving reading.

Print for different purposes

There are examples in this classroom of children using print in a variety of subject areas. The major use of print seems, however, to be as a source of direction. Both the Maths group and the Language group are using the print on their worksheets as a guide to what they have to do. Nobody in the classroom is using print as a source of information. The group which might have been expected to do this most, the collage group, are, in fact, not consulting the book they have available at all. Perhaps the fact that there is a good picture there for them to look at is responsible for this, but it seems a golden opportunity has been missed here to show these children that reading information from a book can give them background knowledge with which to do other things. It is likely that the book they have in front of them has a description of a circus in addition to the picture and, had they been asked to base their collage on this description, they would have gained valuable experience of reading with real purpose. Again the encouragement of children to use print as a source of information seems lacking in this classroom.

The place of other media

Another question which might be asked about this classroom is about the encouragement given to the children to make use of aids to learning other than the traditional school books and worksheets. There is some evidence of the computer being used, in a particular way which I will comment upon a little later, and, of course, we do not know that such things as tape-recorders and video are not used at other times in the school week. However, it does often seem that classrooms do not reflect the experiences of children in their homes, where they will probably be familiar with television, video, tape-recorders, record-players and even computers. These devices all have a valuable role to play in the development of literacy. The point at the moment, however, is simply that if classrooms do not make use of these things then the notion that school is somehow remote from the everyday world is being reinforced. This is a dangerous message which can result in school and the values and skills it attempts to pass on being seen as peripheral and, indeed, largely irrelevant to children's real lives.

 ACTIVITY 6.6

The use of the computer in this classroom is as a flexible type-writer. The children involved are using it to produce a 'best copy' of a piece of written work. The computer is very commonly used in this way and it is worthwhile considering what are the messages about literacy which are passed on by this use. Make some notes about what you feel might be the effects on children's ideas about literacy of using the computer largely in this way. In what other ways might you want to use the computer as a writing tool, and what effects would you hope this might have on children's views of literacy.

COMMENTS 6.6

One of the major strengths of the computer as a writing tool is that it enables even inexperienced writers to produce text which *looks* just as good as that produced by expert writers. Children need not therefore be held back by their presentation and handwriting. The problem with this arises when this presentational aspect assumes priority in the mind of those using the computer to write. There is a great deal of evidence that the aspects of writing which are most valued by primary children tend to be those often referred to as 'secretarial skills'. A more extended discussion of this point and its implications will be found in Unit 8, but, for now, it will be sufficient to point out the dangers of children foregrounding a performative view of literacy as opposed to a functional or an epistemic view. That is, children have a tendency to see school literacy as being chiefly about *getting it right*, rather than as a means of getting important things done or of learning. This over-emphasis upon performing tends to lead to an under-emphasis upon meaning. Form takes precedence over function.

The computer as a writing tool has the potential to challenge this perception fundamentally. Because writing on a computer is provisional, that is it can be changed quickly and easily many times before it becomes a set of marks on paper, it allows writers to think only of what they want to say and to postpone secretarial decisions (how words are spelt, which typeface to select, what line length to use etc.) until later. But in order to work this way, the computer needs to be used as a composing tool, rather than as a transcribing tool. Typing out a previously written story means concentrating only on spelling, grammar and punctuation etc. and reinforces the idea that these are the aspects of writing which are crucial.

3 The teacher's actions

The third source of influence upon the messages about literacy which children get in classrooms is what they see their teacher doing. Their teacher is obviously an important person to them, and what they see her doing can have a far greater influence upon their attitudes and behaviour than may often be realised.

ACTIVITY 6.7

At this point you might like to re-read the very brief description in the cameo of the teacher's actions, and think about what messages she may be passing on to the children about literacy.

- Do you think there might be any kind of a gap between the messages this teacher is trying to convey by the way she has arranged and organised the classroom and the way she chooses to spend her time during this brief snapshot of classroom life?

COMMENTS 6.7

By any token the teacher in this example is clearly an excellent organiser. She has a well-ordered, stimulating classroom, and has developed the ability in her children to work purposefully, often co-operatively, on a varied range of interesting and worthwhile tasks. Because her system is working so well, she is able to spend time giving individual attention to the children in her class, and she has chosen to spend this time on a task highly valued by parents and most teachers alike: hearing children read aloud.

ACTIVITY 6.8

There are, however, two questions we need to ask about the teacher's decision. Firstly, while the teacher is hearing children read, she obviously cannot be doing anything else. She has therefore made the decision that hearing her children read is, at this moment, more valuable than anything else she could be doing. This is a question of values, to which there is no hard and fast answer, but would you agree with her decision? Before answering spend some time thinking about what the alternatives are. What else might this teacher have been doing?

COMMENTS 6.8

Other options for the teacher

There is obviously a range of answers to this question. Assuming that we exclude activities which do not involve her working directly with children, there are several useful things she could have done with each of the groups in the classroom. The Maths group and the shop group may have benefited from having somebody with whom to discuss their activities (assuming they did not lapse into simply answering the teacher's questions, which is a very common result of teacher intervention into small-group activities). Any of the children in the book corner could have gained extra insights into what they were reading by discussing it with a sympathetic adult. She could, of course, also have simply gone to the book corner and read a book herself, thus modelling the kind of behaviour she was trying to encourage in her children. The collage group could have been shown how to use the book they had as a source of information for their picture. The language group could have been encouraged to discuss with each other the work they were doing.

Of course, simply listing alternative things to do is not sufficient. Teachers always have a range of alternatives open to them, and they have to decide from moment to moment which to give their time to. Judging the respective values of these alternatives is not always easy. This brings us to the second question, which is to attempt to assess the effects of what this teacher actually does. How do you think it is likely to influence the views about literacy held by these children?

The effects of the teacher's actions

It is possible that, given a long enough exposure to this activity, the children will come to see this teacher, albeit subconsciously, as a custodian of literacy in this classroom. Although they will recognise the value she places upon reading for pleasure, if her actual time is spent mainly on hearing them read, the children are likely to consider this to be the thing she really thinks is important. By going to a special place to read, the activity itself becomes special. The place they go to is isolated from the rest of the classroom, by being behind the desk. It is of high status, since it is the teacher's place, and it is the control centre of literacy activities in the classroom. The presence on the teacher's desk of what seems to be the only dictionary confirms this. The teacher is the guardian of literacy. Most children come to place a high value on going to read to their teacher. This does not come about simply because of what one teacher does, but experience over several years tends to confirm this for children.

Now, if this activity comes to assume such major importance for children, and indeed for many becomes what reading is really all about, then it matters crucially what it actually consists of. And for many children, as is echoed in this example, what it seems to become is a very passive activity. The child has simply to say what is on the page. There is little incentive to derive meaning from what is there. The child is unlikely to be questioned about what it means. Indeed, the child will often be lucky to get the teacher's full attention. Distractions are common and teachers hardly ever give their undivided attention to readers for longer than a minute or so. The child may get the impression, then, that it does not really matter to anyone whether what she reads means anything. In fact, what will most likely matter far more is whether she can say it accurately. Teachers will often focus unduly on mistakes, without even realising that they are doing it. If the child manages to get through her reading fairly accurately, she will be informed that she 'read well', and, reward given, return to her seat, confirmed in her impression of what her teacher defines as 'reading'.

It is clear that the activity of 'hearing children read' needs some careful thought if it is to be made into a purposeful, beneficial activity.

CONCLUSION

What this Unit has tried to do is to look quite critically (you might think over- critically) at what is taking place in a classroom which most people would recognise as fairly typical. It has not been so much concerned with the outcomes of what is happening here in terms of the learning progress made by the children. The information on which to judge this is not available, although it might be expected that this kind of classroom would produce quite good results in this way. What has been examined is more subtle but, arguably, more pervasive and more important in the long term. Everything that happens in classrooms influences children to some degree, and examined here have been the ways in which the environment and the events in this classroom might influence these children's views on what literacy involves. This is a crucial question, since it is clear that, for anyone, one's attitudes towards what one is doing are a major factor in one's success at doing it.

At this point you should try to spend some time considering a classroom that you know well and trying to analyse it in a similar way to the above analysis of this fictitious, but realistic classroom. You should be able to make a much fuller analysis as you will probably have access to much more detailed information than could be given to you in a simple description.

SUGGESTIONS FOR ANSWERS

Activity 6.3

Imagination is the only limit here, but your list might have included such things as:

- Using newspaper reports as a model for children writing their own reports on events they have studied or witnessed
- Using newspaper headlines as starting points for report writing
- Matching headlines to pictures
- Children producing their own newspapers and making decisions about content, format etc., as well as experiencing interviewing, reporting and proof-reading
- Comparing reports on the same event in different newspapers

These ideas have in common that they explicitly draw children's attention to the ways in which newspapers 'work' as texts. They focus attention on text structures and the choice and effects of language, and can teach children valuable lessons about reading and writing.

Activity 6.4

Texts you might have mentioned include the following:

- Magazines
- *TV* and *Radio Times*
- Letters

- Shopping lists
- Recipe books
- Instruction booklets
- Telephone directories
- Holiday brochures, etc.

Most of these texts will be a natural part of the homes children come from and they will need to feature in classrooms if those classrooms hope to reflect everyday experiences of literacy.

Classrooms as environments for literacy. What messages might they convey?

The texts children read

INTRODUCTION

It is generally true, as I argued in Unit 2, that the role played by certain kinds of books and texts in learning to read has tended, up until quite recently, to have been neglected by educationalists and teachers. But it is possible to argue that it is what you read (or have read to you) that exerts a crucial influence on the kind of reader you become. What you read might well determine how you read, whether you read, and even how you define what reading is and what it is good for.

This does not mean that there has been no debate about the texts that are used for the teaching of reading in school. Far from it: the precise texts used in the teaching of reading have always generated fierce debates in schools. But these debates have by and large concerned the special texts that have been deliberately produced to teach reading. These reading scheme texts are derived from particular sets of theories about how reading should be taught and the debates surrounding them have arisen because these theories are conflicting. Thus, texts have been created to match phonics approaches to teaching reading, look-and-say approaches, linguistic approaches, natural language approaches etc. Such texts are, even in the 1990s, very heavily used in primary schools, apparently being employed by 83 per cent of Year 2 teachers (Cato *et al.*, 1992, p. 23). In this Unit we shall be looking closely at some of these texts and comparing them with other texts which children might read.

Firstly, we need briefly to remind ourselves of some of the lessons we have learnt from research into the nature of the reading process. This was examined more closely in Unit 3. In that Unit it was suggested that reading, by its nature, must be conceived as an interactive process. At this point, it would be worth reviewing that Unit and spending a few minutes on the following activity.

ACTIVITY 7.1

Make a list of the features of text to which a fluent reader attends during the reading process.

Do you think it is possible for reading to take place if only one or two of these features are actually given attention?

Think of some examples in your own reading when you have been unable to use one or more of the features of text. What compensatory action were you able to take?

Research into the reading process

Research into reading, which is described and discussed in books such as Clay (1991) and Adams (1990) has suggested that reading, like other forms of language use (listening, spelling) is a process which is interactive and multi-cued. One way we might explain this is as follows. In reading, although the actual print (the letters, the sounds, the word shapes and so on) does provide us with *some* information when we read, it does not give us sufficient to enable us to do the whole job. When we read we have to get information from a number of sources, and some of these are already in our brains rather than in the print we are reading. These information sources we can refer to as *cue systems* since each of them operates to cue us into various aspects of the representation of language and meaning in written text. There appear to be four major cue systems in reading (Hynds, 1993). These are as follows.

Cue systems in reading

1   *Grapho-phonic*: the recognition of words we already know by sight and the use of our knowledge of letter-sound associations to check words we do not immediately recognise.
2   *Syntactic*: the use of our knowledge of the structures of both spoken and written language in order to make predictions about what we read and to confirm or reject those predictions.
3   *Semantic*: our propensity and ability to 'make sense' of what we read in the light of our previous experience of the world in general and our understanding of the context derived from the text in particular.
4   *Bibliographic*: the use of our knowledge of the conventions and structures of books and other written texts to help predict possible textual patterns.

Reading involves the operation of all these systems simultaneously. If, for some reason, one of them is not operating, reading is more difficult, although not necessarily impossible. Think, for example, of trying to read a text whose conventions and structures you are not familiar with; that is, on which you are unable to use the bibliographic cueing system. For many people such an experience occurs when they are faced with various legal documents, such as contracts. Not being familiar with the genre means that the other cue systems have to work much harder in order to compensate. Another situation might be that you have difficulty in using the grapho-phonic cueing system. Most teachers will be familiar with this as they have generally become fairly expert at reading children's eccentric handwriting and having to rely upon their use of syntactic and semantic content in order to decipher it.

Difficulty in applying one cueing system can just about be tolerated, albeit with increased difficulty. Difficulty with more than one, however, makes reading impossible. Think of trying to decipher a legal document written in poor handwriting! The task would overwhelm most people.

The cue systems are, therefore, interdependent and this fact has several implications for the teaching of reading. The most obvious is that, if children are taught to use only one, or even two, of the cue systems, this will not of itself be enough to make them readers. Several of the popular 'methods' of teaching reading do tend to focus upon one cue system (usually the grapho-phonic) and neglect the others. The 'phonic' method, for example, lays heavy stress upon the teaching of letter-sound relationships and the 'look-and-say' method focuses upon sight words. Such methods risk convincing children, wrongly, that these features are all there is to reading and it is depressingly common to find children struggling with reading who still persist in their attempts to 'sound out' the words on the page. Such children clearly do not need further teaching of phonics but do need to be convinced that reading demands the use of other cues as well. They can, arguably, only be convinced of this if the texts they are given to read draw upon the multi-cued nature of reading.

A closer look at texts

It is only quite recently that ideas deriving from modern literary theory have begun to have a major influence on how we think about texts for children. These ideas focus on the nature of text and the ways in which texts and readers interact. What literary theory has shown us is that books and texts vary enormously in the demands that they make upon readers, and that these variations in demands can exert an important influence upon the way children read. (Meek, 1988; Martin 1989).

One feature of the texts which account for most of the reading experiences of adults is that they are not usually designed to be taken at face value. Most of these texts, for example, stories, poetry, newspaper reports, carry, in addition to their surface and obvious meanings, extra meanings, which vary in subtlety. As an example of this, consider the following text.

 ACTIVITY 7.2

For this text, write some brief notes outlining its surface meaning and then any extra meanings you can detect.

In the beginning there was Adventure. Earnest computer science under-graduates would hunch, red-eyed, over their keyboards solemnly typing in commands. Such pecking brought them the sustenance of further exploration of a world of dungeons and twisty passages, populated by creatures, human and otherwise, which existed only in their under-employed imaginations. And so it was, until one day a particularly under-fulfilled boffin hit on the idea of creating a world in which adventurers could interact (which turned out to be a euphemism for 'kill') with fellow sufferers, *in real time*. And the MUD (Multi User Dungeon to you) game was born.

(Extract taken from an issue of The *Guardian* computers insert.)

What is this text ostensibly about?
Can you detect any underlying meanings? For example, what does the writer feel about the people whose activities he is describing.

COMMENTS 7.2

The passage is taken from a much longer article which is ostensibly describing the development of computer adventure games. Yet it is clear from his choice of language that the author is not really neutral in his feelings about the people involved in these developments. The use of the terms 'red-eyed' and 'earnest' implies that he feels these people spend rather too much time on computers for their own good. Later 'under-employed' and 'under-fulfilled' bring into question the usefulness of the occupations of these people. The linking of 'pecking' and 'sustenance' suggests the behaviour of hens, again not a terribly flattering image. There is also the use of phrases such as 'in the beginning' and 'and so it was', which suggest biblical references, but here these are used ironically. Overall, the tone of the passage carries, not too subtlely, a feeling of making fun of what it describes. To read it as simply a description of what happened would be to miss a great deal of the intended meanings of the author.

Sometimes this under-level of meaning can best be seen by contrasting texts which purport to describe the same phenomena but which are written from contrasting viewpoints. This can be seen in the following activity.

ACTIVITY 7.3

The following are two accounts of the battle of Vegkop which took place in Southern Africa in 1836.

Account 1

This is the account given in the 1980 South African primary history textbook.

The trekkers hurried into the laager and closed the entrance. All around were the

Matabele hordes, sharpening their assegais, killing animals and drinking the raw blood. Sarel Celliers offered up a prayer.

When the enemy made a savage attack, the defenders fired volley upon volley into their ranks. All helped. The women and children loaded extra guns and handed them to the men. After a fierce battle, the Matabele fled with their tails between their legs. The voortrekkers gave thanks to God for their deliverance.

Account 2

This is the account given in the 1988 Reader's Digest *Illustrated History of South Africa,* published in the USA.

The trekkers' first major confrontation was with Mzilikazi, founder and king of the Ndebele. In 1836 the Ndebele were in the path of a trekker expedition heading northwards ... The Ndebele were attacked by a Boer commando but Mzilikazi retaliated and the Boers retreated to their main laager at Vegkop. There, after a short and fierce battle, 40 trekkers, thanks to their guns and an efficient reloading system, succeeded in beating off an attack by 6000 Ndebele warriors. 400 Ndebele were killed and the trekkers' sheep and cattle herds were virtually annihilated.

Try to list the events which you feel fairly sure did happen during the battle of Vegkop in order of their occurrence.

List some of the ways in which different impressions of the battle are conveyed in each account.

COMMENTS 7.3

It is possible to glean a sketchy account of the battle which we can be fairly confident of.

1   A group of Boer trekkers were attacked in their laager by a much larger number of Ndebele / Matabele.
2   The Boers had guns and had a system for rapid reloading which involved their women and children.
3   After a fierce battle, the attack was repelled.

Yet there are some important differences in the two accounts, some of which are only conveyed through their choice of language.

Factual differences

1 Who first attacked who, and why?
2 Why did the Ndebele / Matabele break off the attack? (Because they were forced to by the Boer resistance or because, having killed all the Boers' cattle, they felt they had done enough to ensure the Boers would not survive for much longer?)
3 Who actually won the battle?

Choice of language

1 Why is the name of the tribe apparently different in each account? Which of the names given is most likely to have been the tribe's name for themselves?
2 What effect do such phrases as 'the Matabele hordes' and 'drinking the raw blood' have upon our images of the tribesmen?
3 What effect do such phrases as 'the Matabele fled with their tails between their legs' and 'the voortrekkers gave thanks to God' have upon our images of the Boers?

It must surely be part of our concept of effective reading that readers should be alert to this phenomenon of texts meaning more than they explicitly state. Reading is a multi-layered activity, because texts are multi-layered. If children do not learn to read texts like this then they will miss a great deal of what is going on in texts. They will actually be hampered in their reading.

TEXTS FOR CHILDREN

It is a feature of many books written for children today, picture books especially, that they have this multi-layered quality. Look, for example, at books such as:

• John Burningham: *Where's Julius?*
• Ruth Brown: *Our Cat Flossie*
• Phillippe Dupasquier: *Dear Daddy*
• Anthony Brown: *Gorilla*

These books, and many others like them, have qualities of meaning and narrative structures where the words mean much more than they say (Meek, 1988) and in which pictures and text counterpoint each other. In good picture books like these the pictures do much more than simply illustrate the text. They tell another story alongside that told by the text and it is the trade off between these stories that constitutes the reading. The texts of these books also are often many-layered or multivalent, and contain many examples of innuendo, irony, metaphor and allegory. The texts are 'polysemic', that is, they have hints, secrets, resonances. They make you search and reconstruct; they make you want or need to re-read, to look again, to delve, to discover and re-discover. Children have to experience these things, and learn how to deal with them, because these are the basic skills of accomplished reading and, in many ways, books such as these are the real teachers of reading.

If children are deprived of book experiences like this, then they may never learn the subtleties of reading. If we want children to read, in due course, T.S. Eliot, James Joyce or Shakespeare, with relish and understanding then we need to introduce them early on to multi-layered and polysemic texts of the power of *Our Cat Flossie, Where's Julius?* and the rest.

This criterion for children's early reading texts is, of course, a very demanding one. It naturally leads onto an examination of the kinds of texts which are commonly used in the teaching of reading, that is reading scheme books.

For the next activity, you will need to have access to some of the books from a variety of reading schemes. Those you might look at include:

- *Reading 360* (Ginn)
- *The Reading Tree* (Oxford)
- *One, Two, Three and Away* (Collins)
- *Storychest* (Nelson)
- *All Aboard* (Ginn)
- *The Book Project* (Longman)
- *Pathways* (Collins)
- *The Flying Boot* (Nelson)

 ACTIVITY 7.4

Use the following headings to make an assessment of at least two reading schemes.

- *Name of scheme*
- *Intended pupils* (age, reading level, interest level)
- *Overall impression* (presentation, illustrations, format, print style)
- *Content*
  - linguistic (basis, e.g. phonics, look-and-say, natural language etc.)
  - story lines (likely interest to intended audience? cultural bias? are they real stories, with real plots?)
  - development (does it foster helpful strategies? does its development seem appropriate? what theory of the reading process does it seem to be based upon?)
  - literary quality (can any of the texts be described as polysemic? are children likely to want to re-read these books?)
- Any other comments

It is not my intention here to make pronouncements on the quality (or lack of it) of reading scheme books. Instead, I shall offer for consideration a series of statements made about reading scheme books by Jeff Hynds, one of their most trenchant critics (see Hynds, 1993).

As you read each statement, consider it against your own impression of the reading schemes you have analysed in the previous activity.

A VIEW OF READING SCHEMES

1   'Most of the books and texts in the schemes are rather nebulous and unexciting, and often relatively meaningless. The language is usually pedestrian and unadventurous.'
2   'Scheme books tend to lack variety ... So quite commonly all the books look the same and feel the same, and are the same size, and use the same kind of layout and print.'
3   'The schemes manifestly lack books with polysemic texts, with layers of meaning, implications and secrets.'
4   'The schemes do not envisage or encourage repeated re-readings of favourite books ... The implication is that having finished one book, you move on the next one.'
5   'Many of the texts are ... extremely repetitive, frequently at the expense of meaning.'
6   'The texts are ... hard to read normally, in a multi-cued way.
    (a) There is weak syntactic cueing, because the language is not like normal uses of written or spoken language.
    (b) There is weak semantic cueing, because meaning is frequently slender, limited or even confusing.
    (c) There is weak bibliographic cueing, because picture-text relationship, layout, print arrangement etc. can be misleading.
    (d) On the other hand there is extreme graphophonic over-cueing with repeated words, letter groups, short patterned lines, etc.'

Hynds's argument is that reading scheme books generally do not encourage the development of a multi-cued and multivalent approach to reading. It is fair to say, however, that his comments were written before the publication of four of the eight schemes listed above and one would guess that educational publishers have been listening to the kinds of criticisms which Hynds and many others have made about scheme books. Newer schemes may, therefore, offer substantial improvements in the areas Hynds identifies. Naturally schools and teachers themselves will have to make their own decisions about these issues.

CONCLUSION

In this Unit we have looked at some of the qualities we might hope to find in texts written for children to read and to learn to read. A key point which has emerged is the multi-layered nature of texts in the world outside the school classroom. If our teaching is to help children deal effectively with multi-layered texts, then arguably the texts they are introduced to in school are a crucial element in this. We need, perhaps, to be much more critical about the nature of the texts we use in school than we have been accustomed to be in the past.

The texts children write

INTRODUCTION

A question often asked by teachers concerns the kinds of writing they should ask or encourage their children to do. Behind this question is a feeling, quite commonly held, that children are often not sufficiently extended in the range of writing they do, and a recognition that they should be writing more than the ubiquitous 'story'. In this Unit we shall examine the range of writing which we might expect of primary children, and attempt to set this range into a coherent framework. We shall begin by looking at the somewhat one-sided picture of writing which we have inherited from past enthusiasms.

THE NEED FOR BALANCE

Writing 1971: a true story

Playtime has just finished and the class of third year junior children are drifting back into their classroom. Their teacher, Mr Greene, is nowhere to be seen, so the children carry on talking amongst themselves. Some get out their books and begin working or reading. Suddenly the door of the classroom stock cupboard bursts open and out springs a figure with the head of a gorilla. The figure leaps round the classroom, making monkey noises, and beating its chest. Several children scream, obviously very frightened. Others look puzzled and then begin to grin. A few laugh uproariously. After a while the figure stops moving around, and removes its head. It is Mr Greene, the class teacher, of course. He calms the class down and then begins to ask them questions about how they felt. Were they frightened? Did they feel brave? What would they have done if it had been a real gorilla? As the children talk about their feelings, he jots words and phrases on the blackboard. 'Terrified', 'petrified', 'fierce', etc. After ten minutes or so, he stops asking them questions, tells them to get their creative writing books out, and suggests they write a story about a meeting with a fierce gorilla.

The creative writing movement

The above account (names changed to protect the guilty) represents one extreme of what was a very influential school of thought about writing in the late 1960s and early 1970s. The 'creative writing' movement encouraged teachers to stimulate, at almost any cost, their children to write from their real feelings. Teachers burnt pieces of paper, banged drums, brought in mysteriously shaped pieces of driftwood and big black spiders in jars, to get a reaction from their children which could then be expressed in writing peppered with colourful adjectives and adverbs. It was the approach satirised brilliantly by Gareth Owen in his poem, 'Miss Creedle teaches creative writing'.

> 'This morning,' cries Miss Creedle,
> 'We're all going to use our imaginations,
> We're going to close our eyes 3W and imagine.
> Are we ready to imagine Darren?
> I'm going to count to three.
> At one, we wipe our brains completely clean;
> At two, we close our eyes;
> And at three, we imagine.
> Are we all imagining? Good.
> Here is a piece of music by Beethoven to help us.'

 ACTIVITY 8.1

The above remarks about 'Creative Writing' might be read as extremely cynical and dismissive of any value there may have been in the activity as it has been described here. Yet there were many positive aspects to the Creative Writing movement. It would be worth spending some time at this point considering the positive and negative points of a movement which did have an immense impact upon teaching practice.

What do you think the positive aspects of the Creative Writing movement might have been?

What do you feel were the problems?

COMMENTS 8.1

The creative writing movement seems to us now to be excessively restrictive of what was defined as 'good' writing (every noun has to be accompanied by three adjectives, etc.). It is important to note, however, that in its time it was seen as a positive move away from the limited nature of what most children experienced as writing. One of the important contrasts the movement made was between the writing commonly asked of children in school and this exciting, more involving writing. If children's experience of writing was limited to the filling in of blanks in sentences from textbooks, or other such low level tasks, then the advocates of creative writing had a point.

One of the problems with the movement is now seen to be its use of terms. 'Creative writing' was defined by Sybil Marshall (1974) as, 'the use of written language to conceptualise, explore and record experience in such a way as to create a unique symbolisation of it'. It would now be recognised, however, that there are many different types of writing which do this, all of which could be classed as 'creative'. Interest in children as creative language users in their own right stemmed from the ideas of Chomsky on language acquisition, and it is now recognised that all writing, unless actually copied word for word, is creative, in that it is a unique expression of meaning. 'Creative writing', therefore, is only one type of writing which children can experience. There are many others which need equal attention, and the work in the 1970s of James Britton on classifying types of writing was inspired partially by a recognition of the need for children to gain experience of information-based writing as well as the more personal and poetic.

TOWARDS A BALANCE

The range of types of writing in which we might involve children will be discussed later in the Unit. It is difficult, however, to achieve a real balance in writing in the classroom, partly because what that balance should consist of is problematic. As an indication of the type of balance which might be typical in schools at present, the fourteen class teachers in a junior school were asked to keep diaries for a period of a month of all the writing they asked their children to do. This writing was analysed into types using very broad categories, which were: Narrative, Poetry, Descriptive, Reporting, Personal, Letters, Recording, Instructions, Note-taking.

ACTIVITY 8.2

Before examining the results of the school survey described here, it would be useful for you to think back over the past week or so of your own work with children. Make tally marks against each kind of writing which you have asked your children to engage in and use these figures to work out the frequency by percentage of each type of writing in your classroom.

Writing type	Tally	Frequency %
Narrative		
Poetry		
Descriptive		
Reporting		
Personal		
Letters		
Recording		
Instructions		
Note-taking		
Other		

Do these results surprise you at all? What implications might you take from them for your future teaching practice?

 COMMENTS 8.2

For comparison, the percentage of each type of writing found in the school survey is given below in descending order of frequency. Remember that these figures are an amalgam of the individual writing provisions made by fourteen teachers over the period of a month.

Writing type	Frequency %
Narrative	51
Poetry	12
Descriptive	10
Reporting	7
Personal	6
Letters	5
Recording	5
Instructions	2
Note-taking	2

Clearly there are some problems of precise definitions here, and people will disagree about just how to classify the types of writing they include. Nevertheless the table makes revealing reading. The absolute priority of narrative (stories) is clear and will probably be recognised by primary teachers. The low emphasis placed upon factual writing will also be recognised as fairly common. The absence of forms of writing such as notices, advertisements, and arguments will likewise cause little surprise. It is fairly clear that the balance here is heavily biased towards one form of writing, and that, if this picture is reflective of practice at large, there needs to be some attention to correcting this imbalance. There is, however, no easy prescription to be had as to what might be an appropriate balance. It is really only possible to explore the range of types of writing which might be included within that balanced diet.

DEVELOPING A FRAMEWORK

Perhaps the first step towards establishing what a balanced diet of writing for children would look like is to develop a classification of writing types. Several attempted classifications are available, each with its attractions and adherents. One very influential classification has been that put forward by James Britton and used as the basis for much work on writing emanating from the Schools Council *Writing across the Curriculum* Project in the early 1970s.

Britton's model sees writing styles and functions in terms of a continuum with extremes at either end. For Britton, however, the beginnings of writing are in the central category: the expressive, which he relates closely to the way children and adults use speech. Expressive writing, which Britton sees as the natural form of writing for children, is writing very close to speech in its structures, vocabulary choice and rhythms. In adults it can perhaps best be illustrated by the example of a letter to a close friend. Its relationship to 'gossip' is explicitly pointed out. This 'chatty' style of writing is what children find easiest, precisely because it is closest to the way they speak, and they will often use it even when the teacher may wish them to write in a more impersonal manner, say when reporting an experiment in science. As they grow in experience of writing and meeting the demands of various audiences, so their ability to differentiate styles of writing will increase. 'Expressive writing ... is the seed bed from which more specialised and differentiated kinds of writing can grow – towards the greater explicitness of the transactional or the more conscious shaping of the poetic' (Martin *et al.* 1976).

Transactional writing is the writing found in reports (the adult writing to his solicitor, for example). It is writing done for the sake of communicating information and is usually highly impersonal. Reports, records, notices and instructions all generally demand this type of writing. Although Britton sees this type of writing as being neglected in terms of preparation in the primary years, he is at pains to point out that much of the writing demanded of children in secondary schools is of this type. He sees a gradual shift in children from the expressive to the transactional and recognises that expressive writing will persist in many children when the situation ideally demands a more impersonal style.

At the opposite end of the continuum, poetic writing implies concentration on the form and shape of the writing. This again will develop from expressive writing as children begin to realise the effects of their choice of words or forms of expression, but the two styles will overlap for a considerable time. Poetic writing is not only to be found in poetry. Very often children will begin to give their narrative writing a definite shape; at a very simple level using conventions such as 'Once upon a time ...' is making their writing more 'poetic'.

For all its wide influence, this model of writing has received some very heavy criticism. Although, as Roger Beard has argued (Beard, 1984), it is intended as a classification of the functions of writing, in practice it has been widely used as a way of classifying writing according to form. Beard suggests an alternative model which focuses more explicitly upon the aims of writing as a means of classification, and Beard's influential book has done much to popularise this model.

Kinneavy characterises communication as taking place within a context with three major reference points, each of which form one point of the triangle, the message or content of the communication being in the centre (see Figure 8.1). The model, of course, applies equally to forms of communication beyond writing.

Beard goes on to suggest that a classification of writing according to its aims might be arrived at by focusing in turn on each of the four elements of the model. Thus writing which is chiefly done with the needs of the writer in mind might be said to have expressive aims; that is, be attempting to clarify ideas and feelings in the writer himself. This is not quite the same as 'expressive' writing in the Britton model which, although it does have an important element of self-clarification, also refers to a particular style of writing.

Similarly writing focused on its audience will have the aim of influencing that audience to some degree and might be said to have persuasive aims. Writing which refers very powerfully to the world at large can be said to have referential aims, and will broadly coincide with transactional writing in Britton's system. Finally, writing which focuses specifically on the shape of the text itself might be said to have literary aims (see Figure 8.2).

Obviously there will be a great deal of overlap with any individual piece of writing. A poem, for example, might have expressive aims for its author as it is a vehicle for the expression of deep feelings, but it will also have literary aims, being written in a very particular form which makes its own demands. Nevertheless there are certain forms of writing which seem to fit naturally into any of the four categories given by the model,

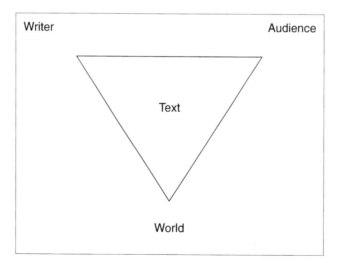

Figure 8.1 Kinneavy's communication triangle
Source: Beard (1984)

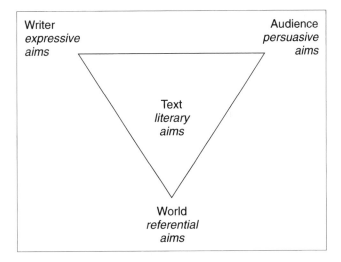

Figure 8.2 Writing aims
Source: Beard (1984)

and it seems a very useful model to take as a basis for ensuring a range of writing experiences.

A RANGE OF WRITING

Using this model enables us to begin to list and develop writing purposes and styles to inform a concept of range. The following list represents only a starting point in this and you will be able to add several ideas to each part of the list.

Writing with expressive aims

There is a range of writing which children can do which will satisfy the aim of expressing their feelings.

Diaries

Some children may find the idea of a personal diary very intriguing, and may use it as the kind of confessional which it can become for adults. Others will not take to this idea, and there is little point in forcing them.

For those children who do wish to write a diary, the encouragement of the teacher will be vital. This should take the form of support and acceptance rather than any sort of coercion, and it should be clear to the children that the teacher will only read what they write if invited to. This is not the kind of writing to mark. Sometimes the diary might develop, if the children wish it, into a dialogue with the teacher, as the teacher responds to what the children say with his/her own personal remarks.

News

A more formal kind of diary writing is the very popular writing of 'news', either daily or at other regular intervals. There is no doubt that this writing can be of immense benefit in the early stages, especially if combined with the idea of dialogue journals, and many teachers will very profitably use children's news writing as a means of developing the beginnings of reading as well as writing. The problem with news writing is that it can very easily become stale and uninspiring. It is sad indeed to find Year 5 and 6 children still spending every Monday morning writing about what they had for lunch on Saturday and who they played with on Sunday, especially as there as so many other exciting ways they can write using their personal lives as source material.

Anecdote and narrative

Anecdote, which with extension becomes narrative writing, is the basic way children use of expressing their experiences. So powerful is it that it is common to find children using anecdote in what to adults seem inappropriate places. Anecdote and narrative are also the most popular types of reading material with children. A very significant trend in research and developments in the field of children's language development has been the increased recognition of the power of stories and storying. It is clear that this form of language use has great potential, and it should be encouraged in children's writing.

This does not mean that children should be set writing tasks such as 'Write an anecdote about ...', but rather that the use of anecdote in all forms of writing should be accepted as beneficial rather than simply an immature means of expression.

Intensive writing

Because of the dissatisfaction expressed earlier with the term 'creative' writing, an earlier label used by writing pioneer Margaret Langdon (1961) has been preferred for what is still a useful form of writing. For all the criticisms made earlier of its excesses, there is still value in the kind of writing which asks children to express their feelings in response to a stimulus.

Stimulus can come from many sources, such as pictures, objects, music, poems, stories, and many children can be stimulated to write on the basis of, 'What does this make you feel?', 'What would you have felt if you were there?' Although this kind of writing can produce excellent results, teachers often find the results disappointing. There are two points worth bearing in mind here. Firstly, children will often write very unevenly, especially in this open-ended task, and so may produce one or two telling phrases only amid surrounding banality. Secondly, it is extremely difficult to write like this to order. Adults, put into the situation that children are in when doing this kind of writing, would also sometimes find it hard to be inspired. If this kind of writing is to be done, then there really should be some way for children to opt out if they are not particularly moved by the stimulus.

Writing with literary aims

In several types of writing which children can do the emphasis will be more on the shape of the text itself.

Stories

This is the most widely produced form of writing in the primary school and obviously overlaps with narrative as discussed above. Here, however, more attention will be given to the shaping of stories. This is necessary because, in fact, a well-constructed story is quite a difficult thing to produce. Many children seem to rush into their stories, beginning with 'One day I…', following with 'and then I… and then he… and then we…', and ending with 'then I went home for my tea', or, perhaps worse, 'I woke up and it was a dream'. Perhaps too much emphasis has been placed upon stimulus points for stories, and too little upon teaching children to structure their stories. The suggestions below relate therefore to teaching story structure.

There are three parts to a good story: a beginning which immediately involves the reader, a middle which carries the story along with a strong line, an end which sums up and further stimulates.

Developing good beginnings to stories probably needs a great deal of example from the teacher. Children can be read stories with exciting beginnings, the teacher can give them some ready-made ones to start them off. Crucial to the success of this will be the provision of time to discuss explicitly what makes a particular beginning exciting and involving.

For beginnings and middles alike there is a great value in getting children to pre-plan their stories, perhaps by using the flow diagram technique. This might be tried out first on stories they know well. For example:

To encourage thought about endings children might be read stories and invited to speculate on endings for them. They might also be asked to write stories with happy, sad, funny endings etc. This will encourage them again to plan their stories so that the ending does not become a simple afterthought.

To develop the ability to think about structure children might be given more opportunities to discuss their stories with each other with structure explicitly in mind.

What these suggestions have in common is that they give explicit attention to what previously may have been unconsidered features of stories. The more children are able to discuss openly aspects of structure, the more likely it is that they will be able to retain full control over their own use of these aspects. This applies equally to all forms of writing.

Poetry

Children's poetry is often considered purely expressively as simply written emotion. Consequently much of it is not really poetic at all, but more like a stream of consciousness, which happens to be organised into lines. As with stories, children might benefit from further work on structuring poetic expression and explicitly dealing with poetic techniques. This approach has become more fashionable, particularly through the studies of Sandy Brownjohn (1980). Brownjohn's work focuses on the use of poetry games and conventions, and has been criticised for encouraging formula poetry. However, the children's examples she uses to illustrate her ideas, and the results many teachers have obtained by using her methods suggest that the straitjacket of form can often heighten expression rather than narrow it. Poetry has, after all, been likened by one celebrated poet to tennis: not much good without a net!

Jokes and riddles

Jokes and riddles are forms of writing which have definite shape to them. They appeal greatly to children who need little persuasion to write them down for others to share. They are, however, probably the one form of writing which will actually be spoiled if discussed. Nevertheless children will revel in finding new variations to the formulae, and will collect 'Knock, knock' jokes, 'Doctor' jokes, limericks etc., thereby developing their understanding of the formulae, and their appreciation of words as a source of fun at the same time.

Writing with persuasive aims

Persuasive here means having an influence upon the reader of the writing, and this type of writing has generally been greatly neglected in schools. There are, however, several possibilities for it.

Advertisements

Children are exposed to a great deal of advertising material out of school, much of it aimed specifically at them. It is generally held that we would like them to be more resistant to this form of persuasion, but little is often done in schools to develop any resistance. One of the ways of doing this is to increase their awareness of the techniques used in advertising by getting them to plan, design and write their own advertisements.

This work could begin by the children looking at a range of advertisements and discussing what makes them attractive and why they might persuade people to buy what they are advertising. They might then choose a product, real or imaginary, to advertise, and plan an advertising campaign for this product. This might be for something like the school magazine, or something more general like children's story books. The campaign might include such things as posters which would need to be designed bearing in mind the characteristics of the intended readers, the information it is intended to convey, and the balance of the poster design.

Letters

Most children are taught how to write letters, but often this is done through exercises which do not have a real outcome. This is a pity as there are many occasions on which letters need to be written and really sent to their destinations in which children can play a greater part. These include:

* Letters to parents requesting party food, giving information about school trips, advertising school concerts etc.
* Letters to organise class visits
* Letters to various organisations requesting information, or presenting arguments, and so on

Arguments

The HMI survey of primary schools in England (DES, 1978) claimed schools gave little opportunity to children to write developing an argument. This is, of course, partly because it is a difficult way to write, even for adults. Children can produce worthwhile work of this type, however, if they are really motivated. As an example of this, this piece of writing from a third year junior child shows that children can become impassioned enough about a subject to write to try to influence people (Figure 8.3).

Writing with referential aims

Transactional writing or writing to get things done probably occupies most of the writing time of the majority of adults, yet it often did not figure largely in the writing diet of primary school children. Yet there are many possibilities for this kind of writing which arise directly out of children's experiences in school.

Reporting

There are many occasions on which children can use writing to record events they witness, and to communicate these events to other people. They can write reports on science experiments, class trips, school sports fixtures, favourite stories and so on. Some of this writing may be done for the special purpose of class or school newspapers, but most will probably be a normal part of school experience. There is, however, little point in anyone

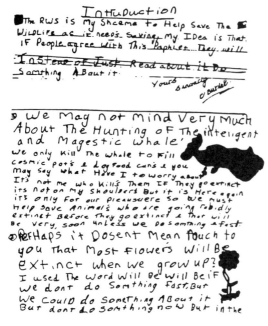

Figure 8.3 Persuasive writing

writing a report unless someone else reads it, so care should be taken to ensure that this writing reaches its audience. This will also give the opportunity for valuable feedback as the audience comments on the appropriateness of the report they read.

Notices

The writing of notices makes special demands upon writing abilities. The search for eye-catching, pointed key words can provide children with useful insights into the effects of language. Schools are often full of notices about things ranging from looking after class pets to advice about road safety. Many of these notices could, of course, be written by children themselves. One useful idea is the establishment of a school or class notice board, whose contents can be chosen, commissioned or written by a notice board committee. Items for the notice board could include:

- Notices advertising school events
- School lunch menus
- Dates of school holidays
- Notices about how to look after the school / class pets
- Messages of congratulations, e.g. 'Well done to the school football team for scoring four goals in their last match', or, 'Congratulations to these people for their excellent playing in assembly last week'
- Posters such as, 'Our school looks better, Without your litter', or, 'Don't just stand and

look, Go and read a book'
- Book jackets and information about the week's featured book, etc.

Instructions

Clear, concise instructions on how to perform a certain task are often very difficult to convey. It is often not until you try to give precise instructions to someone else that you become aware of the level of your own understanding. Instructing someone else can actually teach the person instructing as much as it may the recipient of the instructions. Children can therefore get much benefit from writing instructions for their classmates or others. Topics may include: How to play simple party games, How to get home from school, How to play playground games, How to make things (paper aeroplanes, models etc.), How to do certain tasks (use the phone, load a program into the computer etc.)

Other writing tasks

Writing with information in mind can take many other forms of which the following are just a selection.

- Designing questionnaires to collect information
- Taking notes from people talking
- Making notes from books
- Designing short information leaflets on various topics
- Explaining the thinking behind an investigation in maths or science, etc.

There is, of course, a wide variation in the inherent difficulty of each of these tasks.

CONCLUSION

This Unit has examined the range of writing which children might be given experience of in the primary years, and the chief message to emerge has been of the need for a broadening of this experience. It is not intended, however, that the categories of writing discussed here should be used as a checklist for children to work their way through. Writing which is really useful in terms of children's development is not that which is asked of them simply because it is the next thing on the list. Rather it is writing which arises out of children's needs to express themselves in certain ways. These needs may spring from children's personal circumstances, or from his classroom experience. The sensitive teacher will be on hand to assist with and suggest forms for this expression, and may, of course, shape children's classroom experience in significant ways, but it is especially important that writing arises from children's perceptions of what is necessary and useful. At the beginning of this chapter the creative writing movement was criticised for its excesses, but in one thing the proponents of this movement surely had reason on their side. Children are at the centre of education, and good teachers work with and through children, rather than upon them.

Language as text
Structures and variety

INTRODUCTION

The phrase 'knowledge about language' made a fairly spectacular entry to educational vocabulary in the late 1980s, with the politically sensitive *Language in the National Curriculum* (LINC) project focusing thoughts in England onto a topic which has been considered in various ways over many years. In this Unit we shall examine meanings of this phrase and explore some of the ways in which teachers might develop their pupils' explicit knowledge of the structures and variations of the English language. We shall begin by taking a historical look at developments in thinking around the issue.

DEVELOPMENTS IN THINKING ABOUT KNOWLEDGE ABOUT LANGUAGE

There have been several distinct phases in the teaching of the English language to English-speaking schoolchildren. In reaction to a heavily grammar based approach, probably familiar to many of us from our own school experience, English teaching in the 1970s changed its name, at least in primary schools, to language development, and became much more concerned with the ways children used language than with what they explicitly knew about it. Children's awareness about how language worked was assumed to be developed intuitively from an extended experience of using language. The important aspect of this awareness was claimed to be, not knowledge about the forms of language, but sensitivity towards the functions of language and its effects upon others.

the development of awareness does not entail the learning of a body of facts about language. It is a process by which pupils come to understand much more fully than before the nature of their own experience as users of language. The degree to which this understanding comes to be formulated explicitly in what they say and write about language depends upon their own capacities and the judgement of those who teach them.

(Halliday, 1971, p. 9)

The next swing of the pendulum was signalled by the HMI document 'English from 5 to 16' (DES, 1984). HMI argued that, as a discrete aim in language development, children should be taught 'about language, so that they achieve a working knowledge of its structure and of the variety of ways in which meaning is made, so that they have a vocabulary for discussing it, so that they can use it with greater awareness, and because it is interesting.' (p. 3) This report had a major impact upon national developments, although causing a great deal of controversy. It is at pains to state that it does not advocate isolated exercises in grammatical rules and that knowledge about language is much wider than this, yet its list of objectives for knowledge about language at age 11 consists entirely of statements about grammar.

Subsequently the Kingman report (DES, 1988) extended the idea of knowledge about language and produced a model of language comprising four elements. These were:

1. The forms of the English language
2. (i) Communication
    (ii) Comprehension
3. Acquisition and development
4. Historical and geographical variation

The report argued that 'Successful communication depends upon a recognition and accurate use of the rules and conventions. Command of these rules and conventions is more likely to increase the freedom of the individual than diminish it' (para. 1.11). It suggested that helping children learn the rules is a 'subtle process which requires the teacher to intervene constructively and at an appropriate time' (para. 2.28). This should happen 'mainly through an exploration of the language pupils use, rather than through exercises out of context … so that explicit statement consolidates the implicit awareness and effective learning occurs' (para. 2.30). This insistence that knowledge about language needed to be taught but was best approached through meaningful contexts rather than isolated exercises was taken up by the later Cox report (DES, 1989) and influenced the contents of the National Curriculum for English (DES, 1990).

It is still true, however, that there are many remaining questions about the kind of language teaching most likely to lead to an enhanced knowledge about language among children. Many people would argue, indeed, that the case for an explicit teaching focus upon knowledge about language has not yet been fully justified. What is the rationale for this?

ACTIVITY 9.1

Jot down some notes at this point outlining some of the reasons why you think it might be beneficial to teach children explicitly about the structures of English.

WHY KNOW ABOUT LANGUAGE?

The documentation leading up to the National Curriculum requirements for English (the Cox report, (DES, 1989)) argues strongly for the place of teaching about language. The argument consists of two strands.

> Two justifications for teaching pupils explicitly about language are, first, the positive effect on aspects of their use of language and secondly, the general value of such knowledge as an important part of their understanding of their social and cultural environment, since language has vital functions in the life of the individual and of society.
>
> (para. 6.6)

The second of these arguments is the less controversial but may still need some elaboration. It rests on the assumption that language is central to individual and cultural identity. In many ways understanding who we are involves understanding how we use language (and how language uses us).

Language and identity

Language closely relates to identity in several dimensions, for example, geographical, gender, ethnic and social.

In the geographical dimension it is well known that it is often possible to identify where someone comes from by the way they talk. Regional variations within English may be accounted for by dialect, in which the variation is in terms of the vocabulary and the grammatical structures employed, or by accent, in which the variation is in pronunciation. The work of Giles (1971) has demonstrated that speakers are often capable of shifting their accents in quite subtle ways depending upon the social situation in which they find themselves. This suggests an awareness of firstly the need to change, and secondly of the particular mechanisms by which you achieve this. Similarly, most people are multi-dialectal (or at least bi-dialectal in that they will command a regional dialect and the standard dialect known as Standard English) in that they are able to make shifts in their patterns of speech depending upon social situation. A Yorkshireman attending a job interview will probably not address the interviewer as 'me duck' although that would be quite common in an informal conversation with other speakers of the same dialect. Again, this ability to switch dialects suggests that the speakers have the awareness of the need to change, that is, of the influence of social context upon language, and of the mechanisms of making the change, that is knowing how one dialect differs from another.

At this point it would be interesting for you to carry out some investigations into the dialects spoken by the children in your present class, and into their awareness of these dialects.

 ACTIVITY 9.2

Make a survey of some of the words used by children with whom you have contact which are not part of your normal dialect. This might include new words which the children acquire from television and other media. Consider whether a familiarity with these words is:

- Essential
- Useful
- Unimportant

to you as these children's teacher.
How might you make use of this knowledge?

 ACTIVITY 9.3

If you have contact with children who have distinctive dialects get them to tape record themselves telling familiar stories using their dialects. Are the children aware they are using dialect?
Suggest that they might re-record the same stories but telling them in Standard English. Are they able to do this? This activity might tell you a good deal about the children's awareness of language.

In terms of gender the association in English of a particular way of speaking with a particular sex is not as strong as in, for instance, Japanese, where males and females have distinct styles of speech available to them. In terms of frequency of usage, however, English female speakers are more likely than males to use such terms as 'Oh dear' and 'lovely', and also to ask more questions, make more encouraging noises such as 'mm', but interrupt and argue less (Crystal, 1987). This fits the supportive, rather than proactive, role women have traditionally been allotted in English society. If these linguistic stereotypes are broken, most speakers tend to notice the fact and its implications which suggests a level of awareness of both the rules and the forms.

 ACTIVITY 9.4

Can you think of any ways in which gender variations in language usage might affect your teaching aims and classroom work?

Gender differences are often thought about in education as problems. Do you think this is true in terms of language variation? Why/Why not?

The importance of language to ethnic identity will be obvious to anyone who has seen road signs written in English in Wales daubed with the Welsh language equivalent. Ethnic groups, especially minority groups, tend to seek ways to distinguish themselves from other groups, and language is an obvious, highly noticeable means of doing this. Many such groups have more than one language at their disposal and switch between them according to the social situation in which they find themselves. As an example of this, consider some 8 year olds who were pupils in a primary school in Cardiff. These children were of Pakistani origin and spoke Gujerati at home and with some of their friends. On occasions at home, and at Saturday school, they learnt and spoke Urdu. They were also learning Arabic for religious purposes, although this was not used conversationally. At school they used English in class and with some of their friends, but, because they were attending a bilingual school, they were also learning, and spoke in class, Welsh. This range is surprising enough in itself, but even more remarkable is that these children did not appear to be suffering from any emotional traumas because of their linguistic situation, neither did there seem to be much interference of one language with another. They rarely mixed the languages they were using, largely because each had a quite tightly defined social context in which it was acceptable or expected. This socially dependent differentiation is quite common and suggests the presence of a considerable amount of language awareness in the speakers.

 ACTIVITY 9.5

Make a list of some of the implications which ethnic variations in language usage might have for your teaching.

The relationship between language and social identity is also fairly clear. English is not in the position of other languages in having two separate standard language forms, one for ordinary conversation and one for special uses, primarily in formal speech and writing. This is the situation in, for example, Greek with its 'High' Katharevousa and its 'Low' Demotic varieties, and Swiss German with Hochdeutsch used for formal purposes and Schweitzer-deutsch used in informal speech. English does, however, have social class distinctions in language which are perhaps more entrenched than in most languages. Most people will have encountered the distinctions popularised by Nancy Mitford between 'U' and 'non-U' usage, according to which it is 'U' (or upper class) to have luncheon with vegetables followed by pudding, and 'non-U' to have dinner with greens followed by a sweet. No doubt the precise, in-fashion terms have changed over the years, but the denoting of certain language forms as 'not quite right for the situation' is certainly still current. In order to survive linguistically, without making fools of themselves, people who move between different social situations (which means most of us in these more socially mobile times) need to have the awareness to recognise the demands of particular contexts and to select the appropriate forms to use.

ACTIVITY 9.6

Can you think of any occasions, in school or out, in which the choice of a language variety has not fitted particular social requirements?

Such occasions might be similar to that arising in a classroom I was teaching in when a 6 year old boy confidently informed me that the poem I had just read him was 'crap'. His class teacher, observing my lesson, upbraided the child with the words, 'Now you know you don't use that playground language here.'

Can language awareness be taught?

In each of these dimensions of language and identity it has been pointed out that language users require a great deal of knowledge about language and its contexts in order to successfully manoeuvre within their linguistic repertoires. People unable to do this are trapped in inappropriate uses which can lead to quite serious social handicaps. Linguistic awareness allows control over the language system as it relates to social needs. The issue cannot be whether linguistic awareness is beneficial or not: this is beyond reasonable doubt. What is at issue, and extremely controversial, is how language users develop this awareness, and whether it can be explicitly taught, as the first argument advanced in the earlier extract from the Cox report claims. Does explicit teaching have positive effects upon children's use of language?

This argument is controversial because it tends to be linked with calls for a return to the formal teaching of grammatical rules about which many teachers are justifiably suspicious and doubt the value of much traditional 'grammar' work in terms of its effect upon children's subsequent use of language. The Cox report admits that 'it is true that it has been difficult or impossible to show any direct cause-and-effect relation between teaching formal grammar and improved writing performance' (DES, 1989; para. 6.8). This is, in fact, understating the position. It is reasonably well established from research findings that instruction in, and knowledge of, formal grammar bears no relationship to competency in language use, as the review by Wilkinson (1971) comprehensively demonstrated. Both Cox and Kingman, however, explicitly reject a return to formal grammar teaching, preferring instead a much broader approach. They recommend that knowledge about language work should cover the following material:

1   *Language variation according to situation, purpose, language mode, regional or social group.* This would cover the usage and forms of dialects, accents and registers as well as the influences of context upon language and the differences between speech and writing. Work of this nature would, it is argued, make children more tolerant of linguistic variety and more aware of the richness of language.
2   *Language in literature.* This covers the use of language for particular stylistic effects, and the implication is that explicitly studying the way writers use language may enable children to incorporate a range of stylistic devices into their own writing as well as increasing their responsiveness to literature.
3   *Language variation across time.* This would cover the ways in which language usage, both

grammatical constructions and vocabulary, change historically. Again the argument is that knowledge of this would make pupils more sensitive users of language.

Although the National Curriculum recommendation is for this material to be taught through meaningful contexts of language use, which seems to make more sense than attempting any isolated teaching, it has still to be admitted that the central point of the argument is not yet proven. The recommendation is based upon belief rather than evidence. The central question of whether linguistic awareness can be directly taught in such a way that it leads to improved linguistic performance, or whether increased awareness is itself a product of broadening experience of language use, has not as yet been fully answered.

WHAT DOES KNOWLEDGE ABOUT LANGUAGE CONSIST OF?

Notwithstanding the rather 'chicken and egg' question of how it develops, it is still necessary to clarify what is involved in language awareness. What knowledge about language would competent language users be expected to have?

Much of our understanding on this topic has come from the work of those concerned with the learning and teaching of second languages, particularly Hawkins (1984). Garvie (1990) gives a useful framework incorporating several types of language awareness. These types will be discussed separately under the headings she gives them.

Linguistic awareness

This refers to a knowledge of the basic components of language, that is, the letters, morphemes and words which can be arranged in varying ways to signify meaning. It also includes the knowledge that these components are manoeuvrable.

    ACTIVITY 9.7

Which of the following words might possibly be English words?

forswink   zbastit   mpopo   glenkin   nguien

How were you able to answer this question? The fact that you can suggests you have a good knowledge about the structures of English words and pronunciation.

Language users have a fair degree of morphemic awareness, that is, an awareness of the smallest elements of meaning contained in words. (As an example, the word 'exported' has three morphemes: 'port', indicating the kind of action implied, 'ex', indicating the direction of this action, and 'ed', indicating the tense of the verb.) You are able to solve the puzzles above because of this morphemic awareness.

Research by Berko (1958) suggested that quite young children were able to successfully complete morpheme puzzles such as those given above. Yet other research by, for example,

Reid (1966), has demonstrated that young children often seem confused between terms such as 'letter', 'word' etc. Two points should be noted. The first is that it is actually extraordinarily difficult to find out what young children know about language. Most researchers resort to versions of simply asking them, but never really know whether children who cannot reply do not know the relevant facts about language or merely cannot express their knowledge.

The second point relates to this and concerns the importance of having a language with which to talk about language. Terms such as 'word', 'letter' etc. are part of a metalanguage which may be an important part of linguistic awareness, but is certainly not all there is to it. Many discussions of teaching in this area seem to confuse knowledge about language with knowledge of this metalanguage. We shall return to this point later in the Unit.

Psycholinguistic awareness

The competent language user not only knows about the components of language, but also the rules for fitting these together. Language is a thoroughly ordered system, or interacting set of systems. There are three major systems.

1   The phonological system according to which:

- certain sounds are more likely to follow others. English speakers do not expect, and find it difficult to pronounce, words which begin with the letter combinations 'mb' and 'zd', yet these would be normal combinations to Zulu and Russian speakers respectively;
- some sounds can be run into one another or missed out entirely. Speakers know that it is permissible to omit the 'o' sound in 'did not', but not in 'Didcot'; and to reduce 'and' to the sound 'n' in 'fish and chips', but not in 'left hand side';
- certain combinations of sounds can be stressed in different ways, which makes a difference to their meanings. Language users learn to tell the difference between 'suspéct' and 'súspect' and between 'cónvict' and 'convíct'.

2   The lexical system according to which words are tailored to play their correct roles in sentences. This involves morphemic change and requires in the language user an extension of the morphemic awareness referred to earlier. Not only can he correctly supply the word in

   'Here is a blonk. Here is another blonk. Now there are two ------',

but he can also carry this awareness forward

   'Yesterday I saw a blonk who was carrying its satchel over its shoulder. Tomorrow I ---- --- two ------ who ---- -- carrying ----- -------- over ----- ---------.'

3   The syntactic system which determines appropriate word orders and allows speakers of English to reject combinations such as 'I not can carry this bag heavy' which, literally translated, would be acceptable in French. So powerful is language users' awareness of appropriate order that it can constrain them to reorder incorrect sequences. Kolers (1973) found that adult readers would often read sentences such as the following, which

had been literally translated from the French, 'His horse made resound the earth', with the correct English order, remaining quite unconscious of the fact.

Kolers also found that when readers made mistakes with words they were extremely likely to retain the word's syntactic function, reading nouns for nouns, verbs for verbs etc., thus suggesting a high level of syntactic awareness. This kind of awareness has also been found in 6 year olds by Weber (1970) and in 5 year olds by Clay (1972). In both cases it was found that when these young readers made mistakes in reading words, the words they substituted would most often be the same part of speech as the original. Syntactic awareness seems to develop fairly early in language careers.

Discourse awareness

The language user also needs to be aware of the rules for the combination of the elements of language at a level higher than the sentence. This means knowing how meaning is carried forward from one sentence to the next, either through connective words such as 'and', 'therefore' and 'however', or through the inter-sentence referencing system which Halliday and Hasan (1976) refer to as 'cohesive ties'.

Crystal (1976) claims that children are able to use simple connectives from about the age of 3 years, and can often sustain quite long discourses this way. 'Daddy gone in the garden – and he felled over – and he hurt his knee – and Mummy gave him a plaster – and he didn't cry.' They may use other connectives such as 'but', ''cos' etc., but it is not until quite a while later (around seven according to Crystal) that they begin to use more complex adverbial connectors such as 'actually', 'although' and 'really'.

Cohesion is the device used in language to refer ideas from one part of a discourse to another. In order to sustain understanding over a long discourse the language user relies upon an awareness of how cohesion operates. There are several ways in which this works:

1   *Reference*: semantic relations achieved through use of words, usually pronouns, to refer to objects or ideas mentioned elsewhere in a text.

    John lifted his bag. *It* seemed very heavy.

2   *Lexical*: relations achieved through vocabulary selection, usually by synonyms or word repetition.

    I like cats. They are such lovable *animals*.
    We live in a house. It's a really nice *house*.

3   *Conjunction*: relations achieved through the use of connectors to show the relationships between statements.

    She was smiling, *but* she did not seem happy.
    ***When* you have finished, we shall leave.**

4   *Substitution*: relations achieved by using one word or phrase in place of another.

    I bought a new car today. There were *several* I could have had.

5   *Ellipsis*: relations established by deleting words or phrases.

Who brought the parcel? The postman (*brought it*).

Little is known about the development of children's abilities to handle these language forms in speech, although it appears that little sophistication in the use of cohesive devices is found before the age of eight or so. The work of Chapman (1983b) confirms this rather late development by concentrating upon the use of cohesion in reading. He found that while an understanding of the use of cohesive ties (the use of pronoun references in this case) was associated with ability in reading, there were still many children aged 13 or 14 who found difficulty with this. Discourse awareness seems relatively late to develop, yet the texts which children in junior and early secondary schools are expected to handle are complex in their use of discourse linking devices.

Communicative awareness

The language user also needs to be aware of the ways in which words, strings of words and full discourse can change depending upon such influences as topic, purpose, situation and audience. Language is usually more than a string of words selected to represent a sequence of meanings for its producer. It is normally intended to have an effect upon another person, that is, to communicate. There are many ways of expressing the same thing, and the way which is chosen is usually that appropriate to the particular situation. Most language users will be aware, for example, of the difference between, 'I do hope you don't mind me mentioning it but I'm afraid you're standing on my toe' and 'Get off my toe, you clumsy lump!', and would respond in an appropriate way. Young children exposed to a variety of language situations naturally learn to make adjustments to their language production. They will speak in a different way to their friends in the playground than they do to their teacher in the classroom, and in a still different way to their teddy bear or doll. Communicative awareness seems to develop relatively early, simply through experience.

Sociolinguistic awareness

This form of awareness links very closely with that just described, and implies an understanding of the influence of social context upon the language used. It extends communicative awareness to include a sensitivity to factors such as status and role which influence the degree of formality in communication and to the factors which determine when a particular style of language usage should be switched to another, more appropriate one. I discussed earlier the fact that most competent language users have a variety of dialects and accent forms at their disposal and make reasonably sensitive judgements about which a particular social situation requires. Most adults do this all the time, simply because not to do so would be to be trapped within inappropriate uses with consequent deleterious effects upon other people's views of them as people. The motivation of social approval is usually a fairly powerful one. Some examples of this would include the development of specialised vocabulary and language structures among teenage sub-cultures, and the exclusiveness of the talk amongst interest groups such as computer clubs. To become full members of any of these groups you have to demonstrate an ability to use an appropriate style of language.

Language variations dependent upon social contexts are usually known as registers. The contexts in which registers are used vary themselves chiefly in their degree of formality. When we visit our solicitor, for example, we are likely to use a different register of language than when we are relaxing with our friends. This register will vary in several ways:

- *Vocabulary*: choice of words and word combinations.
- *Syntax*: choice of grammatical forms.
- *Pace*: speed of speaking.

 ACTIVITY 9.8

Think about the register variations you are likely to use in the two situations of a formal meeting with your solicitor and an informal chat with your friends. Note down some of the differences between these registers under the following headings:

- *Vocabulary*
- *Syntax*
- *Pace*

The matching of register to situation is something most of us do without really thinking about it. We simply use language in the way which 'feels right'. It should be noted that it would clearly be as incorrect to use a formal way of speaking in an informal situation as vice versa. The 'correct' way of speaking is that which is appropriate to the situation. Our ability to sense appropriateness is clearly, however, learned from experience and we would expect speakers with more limited experience to be less skilled at it. Just how early in children's linguistic careers this begins to happen is suggested by a fascinating study reported by Andersen (1990). She recorded the language used by 4 to 7 year olds as they engaged, using puppets, in dramatic play set either in home, doctor's surgery or school classroom settings. Although there was some difference in skill at register switching between the age groups, all these children showed an awareness of the need and the means to alter their choice of vocabulary, syntax, topic and speech pitch to fit the roles they were playing. They showed an awareness of status differences between, for example, doctors and nurses, teachers and children and, significantly, fathers and mothers. Such distinctions were made whatever their personal experience of these situations had been like. For example, fathers were always portrayed as 'in business' and in control, with authoritative voices using many imperatives, and mothers as submissive and home-bound, tending to ask rather than tell, even if the children's own parents were not at all like this. The study suggests that young children pick up register patterns from the language they hear all around them, not just in their homes, and quickly become skilled at making sociolinguistic distinctions.

Strategic awareness

The language user is also aware of a range of strategies which can be adopted when there are problems in communication. If, for example, the person to whom someone is speaking evidently does not understand what is being said, the speaker will often try alternative tactics, such as speaking slower, or using signs. If the speaker himself forgets particular words or phrases he/she will adopt strategies to extricate him/herself from the problem, such as circumlocutions or appeals to the listener's ability to infer. The ability to do these things rests upon two aspects of awareness: firstly a recognition that there is a problem, and secondly knowledge of a range of strategies for dealing with it.

Young children also seem to develop this awareness comparatively early. Garvie (1990) gives the example of a 6 year old second language learner who, when shown a picture of a mouse and asked what it was, substituted the unknown word with a scurrying movement of her fingers and the statement 'He do like dees'. It is probably the case that children only develop this form of language awareness through experience, since they are unlikely to be taught how to deal with language problems of this nature which they might have.

TEACHING KNOWLEDGE ABOUT LANGUAGE

As was stated above, the argument about whether direct teaching about language has any effect upon children's language awareness has not been proven. In the discussion so far about dimensions to language awareness the point has been made several times that young children seem to develop knowledge in most of these areas through experience, that is, simply through being users of language. This is not, however, a conclusive argument for not doing any direct teaching. It is still possible to argue that by bringing language awareness to the foreground in children's minds, teaching might make knowledge more explicit and thereby increase conscious control over language. This is in essence the argument used in the Kingman report (DES, 1988) when it is put forward that 'there is no positive advantage in … ignorance (about the structure and uses of language)' (para. 1.12).

Many of the concepts outlined above could be explicitly focused upon in classroom teaching, and there is no intrinsic reason why children should not find the study of their own language as fascinating as they might find any other topic covered in school. The chief consideration would seem to be to embed such teaching firmly into meaningful and engaging contexts. One example of such teaching might be the discussion of dialect poetry of which there are many examples, ranging from the Caribbean poetry of John Agard to the Lancashire dialect monologues of Marriott Edgar (e.g. 'The Lion and Albert'). Children can be asked:

- To rewrite the poem in Standard English
- To discuss what difference this makes to its impact

In the course of such teaching an extra dimension would almost inevitably be involved. This is the use of language to discuss language. In discussing dialects, for example, children would have to use words to describe differences and particular features. They would thus need to use a metalanguage. This might well include terms like those traditionally associated with formal grammar teaching, such as phrase, sentence, verb or adjective, but would need to be wider than this since it would deal with language functions as well as forms. It would need, for example, to have ways of describing the difference between, 'I'm very sorry to disturb you, but I wonder if you would mind just moving your suitcase a little?' and 'I do wish you would move this. It's really in my way.' It is essential, however, to recognise that such a metalanguage is the means to, rather than the aim of, language awareness work.

CONCLUSION

It is possible to state some general principles which should underlie a direct study of language in primary schools. These follow from the knowledge we have about the role of language in making people what they are, and the fact that, by the time they reach school, the vast majority of children have already acquired more linguistic expertise than they have left to learn. Three principles can be stated:

1   Schools and teachers should be aware of the expertise in language which their children bring to school with them, both in terms of a range of forms and in their awareness of the range of linguistic functions. This involves listening to the children and discussing things with them, but it may also involve more sustained attempts to forge links with local communities and with parents. In much work on language it should be accepted that there will often be children in the class who are more expert in certain areas than the teacher.
2   Schools need to begin to work with their children as they are, rather than as they would like them to be. This means accepting that children bring a great deal of linguistic expertise to school with them and planning programmes to make the most of this, rather than to remediate perceived weaknesses. It also means attempting to create school and classroom environments in which children can feel confident that their language will be respected and is an appropriate vehicle for learning. As shown above, the task which children accomplish by themselves of not only learning the forms of a language but also its pragmatic conventions and variations is a substantial one. It will often be the case, however, that they have learned things about language upon which the school traditionally places little value. Schools need to revise their value systems if this is the case. Language knowledge is language knowledge and it is all valuable.
3   Schools should set themselves the goal of increasing the total language awareness of all their children. This means making language itself a much more prominent feature of classroom work. If children learn from experience then the wider this experience can be, the wider the learning opportunities which ensue. No explicit teaching can take the place of meaningful experience. It might, however, enhance it.

If these principles lead to schools positively celebrating the language diversity within them, rather than either ignoring it, or seeing it as a problem, it is likely that a great many social benefits will ensue as children begin to feel that their contributions to school life are important and valued. Whatever the educational arguments for and against the teaching of knowledge about language, these social arguments should not be overlooked. As pointed out earlier, language is more than a transparent channel of communication: it carries its own hidden curriculum which affects self-image and social relationships in profound ways about which teachers need to develop their own awareness.

Unit 10

From learning to teaching

INTRODUCTION

The role of the teacher naturally looms fairly large in any discussion about the learning of literacy. What roles might the teacher play? How might he/she build upon knowledge of children's learning to act in strategic and effective ways in the classroom. In this final unit, we shall examine these issues and put forward a relatively new model of teaching based on research insights into learning. We shall begin by looking at learning.

WHAT DO WE KNOW ABOUT LEARNING?

Four basic insights into the nature of the learning process have come from research over the past decade or so. Each of these has important implications for approaches to teaching. As each of these insights is described, it would be useful for you to jot down in your notebooks any teaching implications which spring to mind.

1 Learning is a process of interaction between what is known and what is to be learnt

It has become quite clear that, in order to do any real learning, we have to draw upon knowledge we already have about a subject. The more we know about the subject, the more likely it is that we shall learn any given piece of knowledge. Brown (1979) has described this as 'headfitting', by which is simply meant that the closer the distance between what is already known by the learner and the particular information to be learnt, the more likely it is that learning will be successful. Learning which does not make connections with our prior knowledge is learning at the level of rote only, and is soon forgotten once deliberate attempts to remember it have stopped. (Most people can remember times they learnt material in this way, usually as preparation for some kind of test: once the test was over, the information 'went out of their heads'.)

Learning has been defined as 'the expansion and modification of existing ways of conceiving the world in the light of alternative ways' (Wray and Medwell, 1991, p. 9). Such a constructivist approach to learning places great emphasis upon the ways in which prior knowledge is structured in the learner's mind and in which it is activated during learning. Theories about this, generally known as schema theories as they hypothesise that knowledge is stored in our minds in patterned ways (schema) (Rumelhart, 1980), suggest that learning depends, firstly, upon the requisite prior knowledge being in the mind of the learner and, secondly, upon it being brought to the forefront of the learner's mind.

Possible teaching implications (*make notes*).

2 Learning is a social process

Ideas about learning have progressed significantly away from Piaget's purely 'lone scientist' view of learners as acting upon their environments, observing the results and then, through reflection, modifying or fine-tuning their schema concerning these environments. Modern learning theory gives much greater recognition to the importance of social interaction and support and posits a view of the learner as a social constructor of knowledge. In collaboration with others, learners establish:

*   *Shared consciousness*: a group working together can construct knowledge to a higher level than can the individuals in that group each working separately. The knowledge rests upon the group interaction.
*   *Borrowed consciousness*: individuals working alongside more knowledgeable others can 'borrow' their understanding of tasks and ideas to enable them to work successfully. Vygotsky has termed the gap between what a learner can do in collaboration with others and what he/she can do alone, the 'Zone of Proximal Development' and suggests that all learning in fact occurs twice in the learner: once on the social plane and once on the individual.

Possible teaching implications (*make notes*).

3 Learning is a situated process

We learn everything in a context. That is not controversial. But modern learning theorists also suggest that what we learn *is* the context as much as any skills and processes which we use within that context (Lave and Wenger, 1991). Psychologists have sought in vain for 'generalisable skills' and all teachers are familiar with the problem of transfer of learning. Why is it that a child who spells ten words correctly in a spelling test, is likely to spell several of these wrongly when writing a story a short while afterwards? The answer is simply that the learning of the spelling is so inextricably bound up with the context of

Learning is a social process.

learning that it cannot easily be applied outside of this context.

There are many instances of this which will be familiar to most teachers. In one of my own primary classes, for example, I had a boy who was an expert at quoting horse racing odds but could not manage school 'sums' although the mathematical content of these was actually much simpler. Similarly, many tradesmen like decorators, carpenters, plumbers have to perform very complex mathematical calculations as part of their everyday jobs yet for many mathematics would have been an area of some difficulty when at school. Medwell (1993) reports how, in her research into children's writing, she found one girl who showed no evidence at all of drafting or revising in her school writing and showed no awareness of this when talking about her writing. She was, however, the organiser of a club for her friends at home and had produced a written set of club rules which showed a number of signs of having been revised. She had certainly not transferred her understanding from one context to another.

Possible teaching implications (make notes).

4 Learning is a metacognitive process

A good deal of interest has been aroused by the notion that the most effective learners are those who have a degree of awareness about their own levels of understanding of what they are learning. Vygotsky suggested (1962) that there are two stages in the development of knowledge: firstly, its automatic unconscious acquisition (we learn things or how to do things, but we do not know that we know these things), and secondly, a gradual increase in active conscious control over that knowledge (we begin to know what we know and that there is more that we do not know). This distinction is essentially the difference between the cognitive and metacognitive aspects of knowledge and thought. The term metacognition is used to refer to the deliberate conscious control of one's own cognitive actions (Brown, 1980). Numerous research studies have examined the operation of metacognition in the reading of children and adults, that is, how successful readers are at monitoring their own comprehension. Overall, there has been a remarkable consistency in the findings of these studies and the two most replicated results have been that:

1   'younger and poorer readers have little awareness that they must attempt to make sense of text; they focus on reading as a decoding process, rather than as a meaning-getting process' (Baker and Brown, 1984, p. 358)
2   'younger children and poorer readers are unlikely to demonstrate that they notice major blocks to text understanding. They seem not to realise when they do not understand' (Garner and Reis, 1981, p. 571)

Arising from such work there has been a strong suggestion that learning can be improved by increasing learners' awareness of their own mental processes. The aims of such metacognitive instruction have been described by Rowe (1988) as threefold:

1   *To promote learners' knowledge and awareness of their metacognitive activity.* This might be done by, for example, encouraging them to think aloud as they perform particular

cognitive tasks, or by getting them to keep 'think diaries' or logs in which they record their approaches to particular problems.

2   *To facilitate a more conscious monitoring of their cognitive activity.* This might involve such activities as self-questioning (Have I really understood this? Have I written this in the best way?) or discussion of their work with peers and/or teachers.

3   *To encourage them to take deliberate control over their thinking.* This might be assisted by discussing and demonstrating a particular strategy for dealing with tasks such as reading.

Possible teaching implications (make notes).

PRINCIPLES FOR TEACHING

From these insights into learning it is possible to derive some fairly clear principles for teaching.

•   We need to ensure that learners have sufficient previous knowledge/understanding to enable them to learn new things, and to help them make explicit these links between what they already know and what they are learning.

•   We need to make provision for group interaction and discussion as teaching strategies, both in small, teacherless groups and in groups working alongside experts.

•   We need to ensure meaningful contexts for learning, particularly in basic literacy skills. This implies some kind of negotiation of the curriculum for learning. What is a meaningful context for teachers cannot be assumed automatically to be a meaningful context for learners.

•   We need to encourage children to think about and discuss their own learning and strategies for learning. This might imply a more deliberate approach to the teaching of skills such as reading and writing.

TOWARDS A MODEL FOR TEACHING.

Palincsar and Brown (1984) describe a teaching procedure which begins from the principles just outlined. Working with the aim of improving students' abilities to respond effectively to text, they begin by arguing that most attempts to train students to do this have produced rather discouraging outcomes, with teaching apparently having little real impact upon learners' use of strategies for making sense of textual materials and, particularly, on the transfer of these strategies to activities outside those directly experienced during the teaching context. They attribute this failure to effect real change in learners' approaches to dealing with text to a model of learning which sees learners as simply responding, relatively passively, to instruction without really being made aware of just what they are learning and why. They claim that teaching, to be successful, needs to encourage learners to be active in their use of strategies and to understand why, and when, they should use the strategies to which they are introduced.

The model of teaching they propose as an alternative is based upon the twin ideas of 'expert scaffolding' and what they refer to as 'proleptic' teaching: that is, teaching in anticipation of competence. This model arises from the ideas of Vygotsky (1978), who put forward the notion that children first experience a particular cognitive activity in collaboration with expert practitioners. The child is firstly a spectator as the majority of the cognitive work is done by the expert (parent or teacher), then a novice as he/she starts to take over some of the work under the close supervision of the expert. As the child grows in experience and capability of performing the task, the expert passes over greater and greater responsibility but still acts as a guide, assisting the child at problematic points. Eventually, the child assumes full responsibility for the task, with the expert still present in the role of a supportive audience. Using this approach to teaching, children learn about the task at their own pace, joining in only at a level at which they are capable – or perhaps a little beyond this level so that the task continually provides sufficient challenge to be interesting. The approach is often referred to as an apprenticeship approach and most primary teachers will be familiar with its operation in the teaching of reading (Waterland, 1985). In the apprenticeship approach to reading, the teacher and child begin by sharing a book together with, at first, most of the actual reading being done by the teacher. As the child develops confidence through repeated sharings of the book, he/she gradually takes over the reading until the teacher can withdraw entirely.

The distance between the level at which children can manage independently and which they can manage with the aid of an expert is termed by Vygotsky 'the zone of proximal development' and it is, according to the model of teaching which has begun to emerge from these ideas, the area in which the most profitable instruction can proceed. Vygotsky claimed that 'what children can do with the assistance of others might be in some sense even more indicative of their mental development than what they can do alone' (1978, p. 85).

Most of us will have had experience of being taught in this way, even if those teaching us could not explain their pedagogical theory in these terms. I learnt to drive a car by sitting alongside an expert driver who had over-riding control of the driving mechanisms (the pedals) and was operating these, without my knowledge, to make sure I did nothing likely to dent my confidence. I taught my daughter to swim by walking alongside her in the water and holding her around the middle while she kicked and splashed her arms. Eventually I began to let go for seconds at a time, then minutes until finally she set off across the pool entirely unaided.

There has also been a great deal of research into 'everyday' learning which tends to proceed in this apprenticeship manner, such as butchers learning to butch and plumbers learning to plumb. This suggests that the model of teaching has wide applicability and may well be capable of offering guidelines for the teaching of basic literacy to adults who have previously experienced little success. There appear to be four stages to the teaching process implied by the model. These are as follows.

1 Demonstration

During this stage, the expert models the skilful behaviour being taught. There is some evidence that learning can be assisted if this modelling is accompanied by a commentary by the expert, thinking aloud about the activities being undertaken. One relatively simple procedure is that of the teacher modelling how he/she tackles the skills he/she is teaching, that is, reading or writing in such a way that the learners have access to the thought processes which accompany these activities. Tonjes (1988) discusses this *metacognitive modelling* as a way of teachers demonstrating to children the reading and comprehension monitoring strategies which they use and argues that teachers using this approach should concentrate upon modelling mental processes – what they think as they read or write – rather than simply procedures – what they do. Only in this way, she suggests, can children learn strategies which they can apply across a range of situations rather than which are limited to the context in which they were encountered.

2 Joint activity

The expert and the learner share the activity. This may begin by the expert retaining responsibility for the difficult parts while the learner takes on the easy parts, while in some teaching strategies prior agreement is reached that participants will take turns at carrying out sections of the activity. The expert is always on hand to take full control if necessary. One of the best examples of this joint activity is that known as 'paired reading' (Morgan, 1986) in which the teacher (or parent) and the learner read aloud in unison until the learner signals that he/she is ready to go it alone. The teacher withdraws from the reading but is ready to rejoin if the learner shows signs of difficulty such as prolonged pausing or reading errors.

3 Supported activity

The learner undertakes the activity alone, but under the watchful eye of the expert who is always ready to step in if necessary. There is some evidence that this is the stage in the process which is most often neglected and many teachers tend to move too rapidly from heavily supporting the children's work to asking them to work without support. Children can easily flounder if left unsupported too soon, but, of course, there are real limits to the support a teacher can offer individual children. There seems, therefore, to be a need for some teaching strategies which operate at this stage of the teaching process but which do not require constant input from the teacher. We shall look at some examples of strategies like this later in the Unit.

4 Individual activity

The learner assumes sole responsibility for the activity. Some learners will, of course, move much more rapidly to this stage than others and the teacher needs to be sensitive to this. It is, arguably, equally as damaging to hold back learners by insisting they go through the same programme of support and practice as everyone else as it is to rush learners through such a process when they need a more extensive programme of support.

THE MODEL IN ACTION

Reciprocal teaching

A set of teaching procedures based upon this apprenticeship model was designed by Palincsar and Brown (1984) to try to develop the reading and comprehension monitoring of a group of 11 year olds with reading problems. Their approach used what they termed 'reciprocal teaching' to focus upon four activities:

1   *Summarising*: asking the children to summarise sections of text, thereby encouraging them to focus upon the main ideas in a passage and to check their own understanding of these
2   *Questioning*: getting the children to ask questions about what they read, again encouraging them to attend to the principal ideas and to think about their own comprehension of these
3   *Clarifying*: asking the children to clarify potentially problematic sections of text, requiring them to evaluate the current state of their understanding
4   *Predicting*: getting them to go beyond the words of the text to make inferences which they must justify by reference to what they read.

Each of these activities had a cognitive and a metacognitive dimension in that not only were the children working upon their comprehension of the texts (comprehension fostering) but they were also having to reflect upon the extent of their comprehension (comprehension monitoring).

The reciprocal teaching procedure involved an interactive 'game' between the teacher and the learners in which each took it in turns to lead a dialogue about a particular section of text. The 'teacher' for each section firstly asked a question, then summarised, then clarified and predicted as appropriate. The real teacher modelled each of these activities and the role played by the children was gradually expanded as time went on from mostly pupil to mostly teacher.

This procedure was tested on a group of 11 year olds with reading difficulties. These children did initially experience some difficulties in taking over the role of teacher and needed a lot of help in verbalising during summarising, questioning, clarifying and predicting. They did eventually, however, become much more accomplished leaders of the comprehension dialogues and showed a very significant improvement on tests of reading comprehension, an improvement which seemed to generalise to other classroom activities and did not fade away after the completion of the research project. Palincsar and Brown attribute the success of their teaching programme to the reciprocal teaching procedure, suggesting that it involved extensive modelling of comprehension fostering and monitoring strategies which are usually difficult to detect in expert readers, that it forced children to take part in dialogues about their understanding even if at a non-expert level and that they learnt from this engagement.

Meta-reading

As an example of this teaching strategy, here is an extract from some classroom discussion. The class were doing some work on the topic of 'Engines' and the teacher was sharing with them a book about this topic. She began by sharing a photocopied extract from the book with a group of children. She accompanied her reading of this text by a commentary explaining her thinking as she worked with its ideas. Here is the first part of her reading (the words in italics are directly read from the text):

> Now, this passage is called *The Steam Engine*. I hope it might tell me something about how steam engines work and perhaps about how they were invented. I know that James Watt made the first steam engine. I suppose the passage might tell me when this happened. I'll read the first sentence or so. *The power developed by steam has fascinated people for hundreds of years. During the first century AD, Greek scientists realised that steam contained energy that could possibly be used by people.* Oh, it looks like the power of steam has been known about for longer than I thought. The first century AD – that's around 1800 years ago. I'm not sure what it means about steam containing energy though. I'd better read carefully to try to find that out.

During this meta-reading, the teacher was concentrating on doing four kinds of things. She was:

- *Predicting:* looking forward to the information the text might give her.
- *Clarifying:* working out ideas in ways she could better understand them.
- *Questioning:* allowing the text to spark off further questions in her mind.
- *Summarising:* putting the information in the text into a few words.

These four activities were discussed explicitly with the group and written on large cards which were displayed in the classroom. Later, with a different passage, the teacher agreed with the group that they would take it in turns to predict what the passage might be going to be about, to clarify what it told them, to ask questions about what they read and to summarise what they learnt.

Later still, the group were given the task of reading a passage amongst themselves using the same strategies to guide their discussion.

The ultimate aim, of course, was that they would become sufficiently familiar with this procedure for interacting with a text that they were able to adopt it when reading themselves. What they learnt as a social activity would become internalised and individual.

EXTENDING THE SCAFFOLDING

If, as suggested above, teachers have a tendency to withdraw too quickly the support (scaffolding) they offer to learners who are struggling to master new skills, then there may be some use in the provision of support structures which learners can use without the necessity for the teacher to be constantly alongside them. I shall describe here two such support structures, both of which relate particularly to helping readers find and use information from non-fiction texts.

What do I *know* about this topic?	What do I *want* to know?	What did I *learn*?

Figure 10.1 A KWL grid

KWL grids

The KWL grid was developed as a teaching strategy in the USA (Ogle, 1989) and is a simple but effective strategy which both takes readers through the steps of the research process and also records their learning. It gives a logical structure for tackling research tasks in many areas of the curriculum and it is this combination of a simple but logical support scaffolding that seems to be so useful to readers with learning difficulties. A KWL grid consists of three columns (see Figure 10.1), the first two of which set the scene for the reading by requiring thought about prior knowledge and just what the reader predicts he/she might learn from the material to be read. The third column acts as a note-taking space.

Because this strategy begins with the reader's knowledge and then requires them to focus on particular questions, it makes the copying out of large sections from the text very unlikely. Most teachers of junior-aged children will recognise the copying phenomenon as one of their biggest problems in teaching children to read for information, an observation which is probably not confined to that age group.

Writing frames

As a means of scaffolding children's writing, the use of frames has been found to be useful (Lewis and Wray, 1995). These simply give the basic structure for a piece of writing by setting out a sequence of cohesive ties to which the writer supplies the content. Some examples of such frames were given earlier in Unit 4. This strategy seems to be specially useful for children with reading problems. As an example of this, Figure 10.2 shows the writing produced by Edward, an 8 year old with severe learning problems, after discussion with his support teacher (she scribed the first sentence for him). What it suggests is that

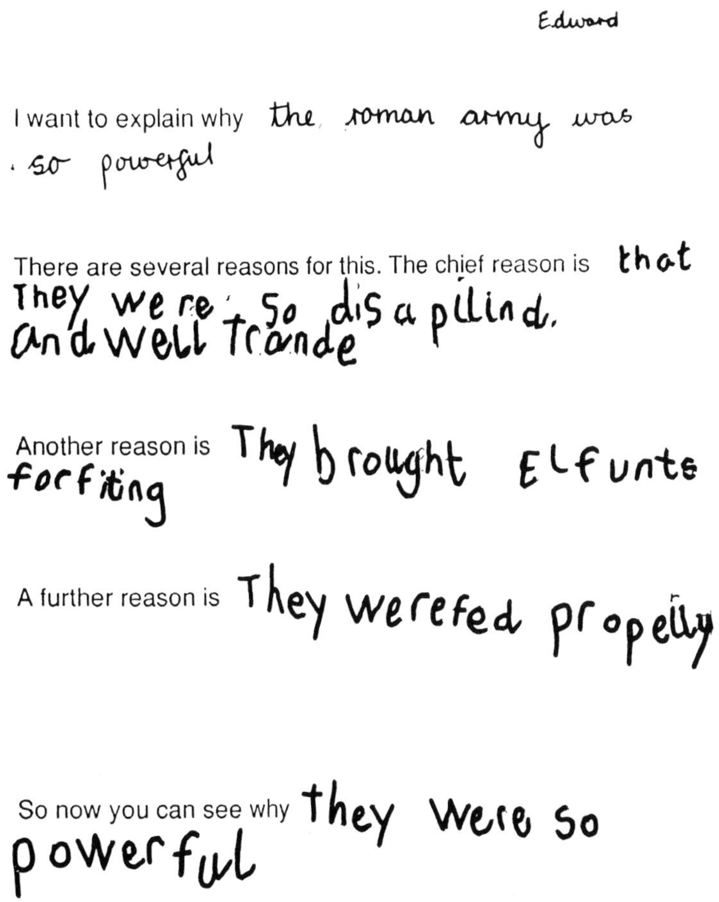

Edward

I want to explain why *the roman army was so powerful*

There are several reasons for this. The chief reason is *that They were so disa pllind, and well trande*

Another reason is *forfiting They brought ELfunte*

A further reason is *They werefed propelly*

So now you can see why *they were so powerful*

Figure 10.2 Explanation writing frames

Edward, for all his problems, had learnt a good deal about the Roman army and had previously lacked only the support to express his knowledge in a coherent piece of writing.

CONCLUSION

Based upon insights about learning, we now have a view about the teacher's role in literacy and language development which appears to command wide acceptance among theorists and practitioners alike. The four part model to describe teaching which was earlier outlined can be used to inform and develop a range of teaching approaches and strategies and clearly deserves serious consideration by teachers.

References

Adams, M.J. (1990) *Beginning to Read* Cambridge, Mass.: MIT Press

Andersen, E.S. (1990) *Speaking with Style* London: Routledge

Baker, L. and Brown, A. (1984) 'Metacognitive skills and reading', in Pearson, D. (ed.) *Handbook of Reading Research* New York: Longman

Barnes, D. (1976) *From Communication to Curriculum* Harmondsworth: Penguin

Beard, R. (1984) *Children's Writing in the Primary School* Sevenoaks: Hodder & Stoughton

Bellack, A., Kliebard, H. Hyman, R. and Smith, F. (1966) *The Language of the Classroom* Columbia: Teachers College Press

Berko, J. (1958) 'The child's learning of English morphology' *Word*, Vol. 14, pp. 150–177

Brown, A. (1979) 'Theories of memory and the problems of development: activity, growth and knowledge', in Cermak, L. and Craik, F. (eds) *Levels of Processing in Human Memory* Hillsdale, New Jersey: Erlbaum

Brown, A. (1980) 'Metacognitive development and reading', in Spiro, R., Bruce, B. and Brewer, W. (eds) *Theoretical Issues in Reading Comprehension* Hillsdale, New Jersey: Erlbaum

Brownjohn, S. (1980) *Does It Have to Rhyme?* Sevenoaks: Hodder & Stoughton

Bruner, J. (1985) 'Vygotsky: a historical and conceptual perspective', in Wertsch, J. (ed.) *Culture, Communication and Cognition: Vygotskyan Perspectives* Cambridge: Cambridge University Press

Bruner, J. and Haste, H. (1987) *Making Sense: the Child's Construction of the World* London: Metheun

Cambourne, B. (1988) *The Whole Story* Auckland, New Zealand: Ashton Scholastic

Cato, V. and Whetton, C. (1991) *An Enquiry into LEA Evidence on Standards of Reading of Seven Year Old Children* London: HMSO

Cato, V., Fernandes, C., Gorman, T. and Kispal, A. (1992) *The Teaching of Initial Literacy: How Do Teachers Do It?* Slough, Berks: The National Foundation for Educational Research

Chapman, J. (1983a) *Reading Development and Cohesion* London: Heinemann

Chapman, J. (1983b) 'A study in reading development: a comparison of the ability of 8-, 10- and 13-year-old children to perceive cohesion in their school texts', in Gillham, B. (ed.) *Reading through the Curriculum* London: Heinemann

Chapman, J. (1987) *Reading: from 5–11 Years* Milton Keynes: Open University Press

Christie, F. (1990) 'The changing face of literacy', in Christie, F. (ed.) *Literacy for a Changing World* Hawthorn, Victoria: Australian Council for Educational Research

Clay, M. (1972) *Reading: the Patterning of Complex Behaviour* London: Heinemann

Clay, M. (1991) *Becoming Literate: the Construction of Inner Control* Birkenhead, Auckland: Heinemann

Crystall, D. (1976) *Child Language, Learning and Linguistics* London: Edward Arnold

Crystal, D. (1987) *The Cambridge Encyclopaedia of Language* Cambridge: Cambridge University Press

Culler, J. (1981) *The Pursuit of Signs* London: Routledge & Kegan Paul

DES, (1978) *Primary Education in England* London: HMSO

DES, (1984) *English from 5 to 16* London: HMSO

DES, (1988) *Report of the Committee of Inquiry into the Teaching of English Language* London: HMSO

DES, (1989) *English for Ages 5 to 16* London: HMSO

DES, (1990) *English in the National Curriculum* London: HMSO

Derewianka, B. (1990) (ed.) *Exploring How Texts Work* Rozelle, New South Wales: Primary English Teaching Association

Edwards, D. and Mercer, N. (1987) *Common Knowledge* London: Methuen

Edwards, A. and Westgate, D. (1987) *Investigating Classroom Talk* London: Falmer Press

Flanders, N. (1970) *Analysing Teacher Behaviour* Reading, Mass.: Addison-Wesley

Garner, R. and Reis, R. (1981) 'Monitoring and resolving comprehension obstacles: an investigation of spontaneous text lookbacks among upper grade good and poor comprehenders', *Reading Research Quarterly*, Vol. 16, pp. 569–582

Garvie, E. (1990) *Story as Vehicle* Clevedon: Multilingual Matters

Giles, H. (1971) 'Our reactions to accent', *New Society*, 14 October

Goodman, K. (1985) 'Unity in reading', in Singer, H. and Ruddell, R. (eds) *Theoretical Models and Processes of Reading* Newark, Delaware: International Reading Association

Graves, D. (1983) *Writing: Teachers and Children at Work* Portsmouth, New Hampshire: Heinemann

Halliday, M. (1971) 'Foreword', in Doughty, P., Pearce, J. and Thornton, G., *Language in Use* London: Edward Arnold

Halliday, M. (1978) *Languages as Social Semiotic* London: Edward Arnold

Halliday, M. and Hasan, R. (1976) *Cohesion in English* London: Longman

Halliday, M. and Hasan, R. (1989) *Language, Context and Text* Oxford: Oxford University Press

Hawkins, E. (1984) *Awareness of Language* Cambridge: Cambridge University Press

Hughes, M. (1994) 'The oral language of young children', in Wray, D and Medwell, J. (eds) *Teaching Primary English: the State of the Art* London: Routledge

Hynds, J. (1993) 'Text and neglect', in Wray, D. (ed.) *Literacy: Text and Context* Widnes: United Kingdom Reading Association

Kolers, P. (1973) 'Three stages of reading', in Smith, F. (ed.) *Psycholinguistics and Reading*, New York: Holt, Rinehart & Winston

Langdon, M. (1961) *Let the Children Write* London: Longmans

Lave, J. and Wenger, E. (1991) *Situated Learning* Cambridge: Cambridge University Press

Lewis, M. and Wray, D. (1995) *Developing Children's Non-Fiction Writing* Leamington Spa: Scholastic

Marshall, S. (1974) *Creative Writing* London: Macmillan

Martin, J. (1989) *Factual Writing* Oxford: Oxford University Press

Martin, N., D'Arcy, P., Newton, B. and Parker, R. (1976) *Writing and Learning across the Curriculum 11–16* London: Ward Lock

Medwell, J. (1990) 'An investigation of the relationship between perceptions of the reading process and reading strategies of eight year old children', unpublished M.Ed. Dissertation, University of Wales

Medwell, J. (1991) 'Contexts for writing', paper given at the European Conference on Reading, Edinburgh, July 1991

Medwell, J. (1993) 'A critical look at classroom contexts for writing', in Wray, D. (ed.) *Literacy: Text and Context* Widnes: United Kingdom Reading Association

Meek, M. (1988) *How Texts Teach What Readers Learn* Stroud: Signal

Morgan, R. (1986) *Helping Children Read* London: Metheun

Ogle, D.M. (1989) 'The know, want to know, learn strategy', in Muth, K.D. (ed.) *Children's Comprehension of Text* Newark, Delaware: International Reading Association

Palincsar, A. and Brown, A. (1984) 'Reciprocal teaching of comprehension-fostering and comprehension-monitoring activities', *Cognition and Instruction*, Vol. 1, No. 2, pp. 117–175

Reid, J. (1966) 'Learning to think about reading', *Educational Research*, Vol. 9, pp. 56–62

Rosenblatt, L. (1978) *The Reader, the Text, the Poem* Carbondale: Southern Illinois University Press

Rowe, H. (1988) 'Metacognitive skills: promises and problems', *Australian Journal of Reading,* Vol. 11, No. 4, pp. 227–237

Rumelhart, D. (1980) 'Schemata: the building blocks of cognition', in Spiro, R., Bruce, B. and Brewer, W. (eds) *Theoretical Issues in Reading Comprehension* Hillsdale, New Jersey: Lawrence Erlbaum

Rumelhart, D. (1985) 'Toward an interactive model of reading', in Singer, H. and Ruddell, R. (eds) *Theoretical Models and Processes of Reading* Newark, Delaware: International Reading Association

Sinclair, J. and Coulthard, M. (1975) *Towards an Analysis of Discourse: the Language of Teachers and Pupils* London: Oxford University Press

Tonjes, M. (1988) 'Metacognitive modelling and glossing: two powerful ways to teach self-responsibility', in Anderson, C. (ed.) *Reading: the ABC and Beyond* Basingstoke: Macmillan

Vygotsky, L. (1962) *Thought and Language* Cambridge, Mass.: MIT Press

Vygotsky, L. (1978) *Mind in Society* Cambridge, Mass.: Harvard University Press

Wade, B. (ed.) (1985) *Talking to Some Purpose* Birmingham: Educational Review

Waterland, L. (1985) *Read with Me* Stroud: Thimble Press

Weber, R. (1970) 'First graders' use of grammatical context in reading', in Levin, H. and Williams, J. (eds) *Basic Studies in Reading* New York: Basic Books

Wells, G. (1987) *The Meaning Makers,* London: Hodder & Stoughton

Wilkinson, A. (1971) *The Foundations of Language* Oxford: Oxford University Press

Wray, D. (1990) 'Text-processing: the implications for literacy', in Potter, F. *Communication and Learning* Oxford: Basil Blackwell

Wray, D. (1994) *Literacy and Awareness* London: Hodder & Stoughton

Wray, D., Bloom, W. and Hall, N. (1989) *Literacy in Action* Lewes: Falmer Press

Wray, D. and Gallimore, J. (1986) 'Drafting in the classroom', *Primary Teaching Studies,* Vol. 1, No. 3, pp. 65–77

Wray, D. and Medwell, J. (1991) *Literacy and Language in the Primary Years* London: Routledge

Wray, D. and Medwell, J. (1994) (eds) *Teaching Primary English: the State of the Art* London: Routledge

Author Index

Subject Index